POLITICAL PHILOSOPHY NOW

Chief Editor of the Series:
Howard Williams, University of Wales, Aberystwyth

Associate Editors:
Wolfgang Kersting, University of Kiel, Germany
Steven B. Smith, Yale University, USA
Peter Nicholson, University of York, England
Renato Cristi, Wilfrid Laurier University, Waterloo, Canada

Political Philosophy Now is a series which deals with authors, topics and periods in political philosophy from the perspective of their relevance to current debates. The series presents a spread of subjects and points of view from various traditions which include European and New World debates in political philosophy.

For other titles in this series, please see the University of Wales website: www.wales.ac.uk/press

POLITICAL PHILOSOPHY NOW

Machiavelli Revisited

Joseph V. Femia

UNIVERSITY OF WALES PRESS • CARDIFF • 2004

© Joseph V. Femia, 2004

British Library Cataloguing-in-Publication Data
A catalogue record for this book is available from the British Library.

ISBN 0-7083-1722-7 hardback
0-7083-1721-9 paperback

Typeset by Mudra Typesetters, Pondicherry, India.
Printed in Great Britain by The Cromwell Press

Contents

Preface

When scientists disagree with one another, they do so most often at the frontiers of knowledge, where growth is taking place; and in the long run a debated question is ordinarily settled by observation, experiment, or some other method that all accept. By way of contrast, the issues that divide Machiavelli scholars will never be resolved to everyone's satisfaction. Interpreting Machiavelli is not like participating in a technical exercise where finality can be confidently expected; it is more akin to engaging in an endless and inconclusive conversation about a topic of deep and unfathomable complexity. Naturally, all readers of Machiavelli believe that the interpretation which they derive from his works coincides with his intentions. But this would be so only if readers were essentially passive in their reception of the meaning originally embodied within his texts. Given the astonishing variety of interpretations to which Machiavelli has been subjected, it is clear that his readers are far from passive: they are evidently projecting their own values or preoccupations on to his works. In some measure this is inevitable. However, an acknowledgement of the fact that Machiavelli is open to a number of legitimate readings does not mean that all readings are equally faithful to the texts.

At present, the literature on Machiavelli is dominated by those who situate him squarely within the Florentine tradition of 'civic humanism' – a tradition devoted to ideals of patriotism, popular government and public service. From this perspective, he was merely developing an established mode of discourse; he was not – as is often supposed – a radical innovator, a herald of modernity, or a pioneer of modern political science. Still less was he an apologist for tyranny. What we have here is a 'sanitized' version of Machiavelli, similar to sanitized versions of Marx or Nietzsche. In all three cases, there is an exegetical tendency to gloss over or even ignore the thinker's more shocking or unfashionable utterances and to accentuate whatever might make him acceptable to progressive and humanistic academics. Thus the Machiavelli who emerges from much recent literature is a 'classical republican', or – to put it into today's language – a communitarian democrat, wedded to peace, popular participation and civil liberties.

My primary motive for writing this book was dissatisfaction with this type of interpretation, which I find misleading and anachronistic (though its proponents generally describe themselves as contextual historians). I accept, however, that those who portray Machiavelli as a gentle republican are reacting against moralistic denunciations of him as an unscrupulous and malevolent precursor of modern totalitarianism. Seeing Machiavelli as an evil genius, as nothing but an illiberal and ruthless calculator of political advantage, is just as misleading as the opposite interpretation. Readers will note that my own view of Machiavelli falls somewhere between the two extremes, neither of which, I shall argue, permits us to grasp the true significance and value of his thought. Exploring Machiavelli's relevance to our own world is the main purpose of this book. It is not an intellectual biography, and I have kept historical details to a minimum. Nor have I attempted to provide a definitive or exhaustive analysis of *every* controversy within the fields of Renaissance and Machiavelli studies. For fear of alienating the general reader, I have had to choose, without much discussion in the text, what seems to me the probable truth on some matters still debated by scholars. I hope all the same that I have succeeded in providing the general reader no less than academic specialists with a fair and balanced picture of Machiavelli's achievement.

Joseph V. Femia,
University of Liverpool, 2003

Acknowledgements

Thanks are owed to a number of friends and colleagues who helped me to clarify my ideas on Machiavelli. Howard Williams, who kindly invited me to contribute this study to the series he is editing, read the entire typescript in draft form and suggested many improvements. My debt to him is great. I am further indebted to Maurice Finocchiaro for reading a couple of draft chapters and offering me valuable comments and criticisms. David Boucher, who read my previous publications on Machiavelli and gave me useful advice on how they could be expanded and developed, also deserves my gratitude. A semester as Visiting Fellow in the Department of History at Princeton University, back in 1997, afforded a superb environment for research and reflection on Machiavelli, allowing me to benefit from the expertise of Maurizio Viroli and Anthony Grafton, amongst others. I am also grateful to the British Academy for supporting this Fellowship with a generous research grant. Finally, my thanks are due to Ros Saunders, Sue Moss, Marie Ferguson and Jo McLellan for producing the typescript with remarkable efficiency.

Throughout this book, I have borrowed material from two of my own publications: chapter 1 of J. Femia, *The Machiavellian Legacy: Essays in Italian Political Thought* (Basingstoke: Macmillan, 1998); and 'Machiavelli', in D. Boucher and P. Kelly (eds), *Political Thinkers: From Socrates to the Present* (Oxford: Oxford University Press, 2003), pp. 139–59. Acknowledgement is gratefully made to the appropriate editors and publishers.

impecunious lawyer, made sure that his son was thoroughly imbued with the great traditions of his native city. Niccolò received a gentlemanly education, studied the classics, and learned to read and write in Latin, without acquiring any particular reputation as a man of scholarship or cultural refinement. Little is known of his early life. He was twenty-five when the first French invasion of Italy took place in 1494, and from this moment Florence entered upon a tumultuous history. In that year, the Florentines rose up to reclaim their ancient liberties, driving the Medici out of Florence and proclaiming a *genuine* republic. This reversion to the more democratic practices of a previous age did not, however, bring civil tranquillity. For the next four years, the city fell under the sway of Savonarola's fierce eloquence and religious fanaticism. Anxious to purify morals, the Dominican friar made it his mission to attack luxury and corruption, and to set the poor against the rich. While the people listened to him, he was all-powerful; but they soon grew weary of his austere and divisive message. In the course of a complex faction fight, the Florentine Signoria, or ruling committee, turned against him and he was burned at the stake. After Savonarola's dramatic fall from grace, and the restoration of more sober governance, Machiavelli, still not thirty, was appointed second Chancellor of the republic. Shortly afterwards, he was given the additional charge of secretary to the influential committee known as the *Dieci di Balia*, the Ten of Liberty and Peace as they were sometimes grandiloquently called, or, more realistically, the Ten of War.

War was the main preoccupation of the restored republic. Foreign armies now invaded Italy with impunity. Spaniards slowly tightened their grip on Naples; the French, bent on conquest, roamed all over the land. Germans and Switzers were also in the field, often for foreign paymasters but sometimes on behalf of the Holy Roman Empire. Popes were trying to unify the anarchic Papal States of central Italy. In the midst of these big wars, Florence was engaged in an interminable little war to reconquer Pisa, which had slipped from the Florentine yoke. The scholarly consensus is that the descent of the French into Italy marked 'a turning-point in the history of the peninsula'.[2] The delicate balance between Italy's five principal states – the Papacy, Naples, Venice, Milan and Florence – was destroyed. As military weaklings, these 'statelets' never seriously threatened each other's existence or mode of government. Their wars, whilst prolonged, were usually fought by mercenaries whose enthusiasm was less than total; casualties tended to be low and large-scale destruction was rare. The French and the Spaniards, with their formidable military machines, wreaked a terrible devastation on Italy, and exposed the parochial nature of its complex political manoeuvrings and chessboard warfare. Battles became bloody and decisive. Once it would take months to occupy a small village, now whole cities were taken in days and hours. The Florence Machiavelli served was therefore vulnerable and in constant danger. Hardly able to subdue Pisa, it stood no chance against the powerful foreigners and was forced – in effect – to 'buy' protection from the French by supporting their ambitions elsewhere in the peninsula. Machiavelli spent fourteen years in the service of this rather weak state. Apart from writing countless memoranda to inform and advise his masters on a variety of subjects, he was sent on numerous diplomatic missions, either to places under Florentine rule or to the governments of foreign states. He seemed to enjoy the diplomatic bickering and haggling that were the normal Renaissance accompaniments of war. His renowned prose-style, his pungent manner of expression, full of cynical and telling aphorisms, was the currency of Italian diplomacy.[3] But while serving the republic, he never found time for systematic theoretical reflection. What he did do was to build up a fund of material later to be distilled in his famous works. His apparent esteem for Cesare Borgia, for example, was based on direct experience. As commander-in-chief of the Papal army, the Duke of Valentinois (or Valentino, as Borgia was known in Italy) took delight in committing his foul deeds when the Florentine emissary was in his presence. Machiavelli watched, fascinated, while the notorious monster lured some of his mutinous subordinates to a peace conference, invited them to a banquet to celebrate their renewed friendship and (when they arrived unarmed and unescorted) had them seized and murdered. Machiavelli was also there at Cesena when the departing Borgia left behind him in the town square a bisected body with a block of wood and a bloody knife beside it. The body was that of Ramiro d'Orco, his faithful servant in the Romagna, who had earned the enmity of the local people by suppressing dissent in the most vicious way. When the Duke wanted to impress the populace or gain political advantage, his loyal friends were no safer than his sworn enemies. In his dispatches, Machiavelli noted the effectiveness of Borgia's brutal virtuosity, and later made it clear that statesmen could derive useful precepts from such behaviour. But Machiavelli's official correspondence also recognized that the serial untrustworthiness of the Duke had its drawbacks, and that he had benefited from good fortune (for example, being the who demanded the deposition of the *gonfaloniere*, Piero Soderini. These demands were refused, and the Spanish army advanced for the kill. When they attacked Prato – a Florentine protectorate – Machiavelli's militia reacted like frightened rabbits, abandoning the city to a brutal sack. The increasingly unpopular Soderini regime was now thoroughly discredited and the Medici party within Florence insisted on the *gonfaloniere*'s resignation. Soderini took flight, the constitution was radically changed, and the Medici came back to rule Florence – protected by a column of Spanish pikes. The republic was no more. Machiavelli was deprived of all office and banished from Florence itself, but compelled, under a surety of a thousand gold florins, to remain within Florentine territory. Worse was to come. In early 1513, an anti-Medici conspiracy was uncovered. The comically inept conspirators had compiled a list of 'likely supporters' and left it lying about. Alas for Machiavelli, his name was on the list, and he was arrested and subjected to four turns of the rack. He confessed nothing because he knew nothing; and when the matter came to trial, his sentence was no worse than a fine. But as suspicion now hung over him, the Medici showed no inclination to revive his political career. Other servants of the republic found their way back into public employment; Machiavelli retreated to his country house seven miles south of the city and struggled to come to terms with his enforced retirement.

Diplomacy's loss was posterity's gain. The ad hoc observations of the political participant gave way to a more general theoretical examination of the underlying realities of political action. A miserable soul, who continued to follow political affairs with the painful longing of a spurned lover, Machiavelli would dress up in courtly attire and spend each evening in the company of ancient authors, whose texts he scoured for inspiration. Despite (or because of) his obsessive behaviour, he succeeded in producing two classics of political thought: *The Prince*, completed in 1513, and the *Discourses on Livy*, composed from 1513 to 1517. Neither was actually printed until 1531, four years after his death. In 1520, his repeated attempts to gain the favour of the Medici finally yielded fruit in the form of a commission from Cardinal Giulio de' Medici to write a history of Florence, which was published in 1527, the year of his demise. The *Istorie fiorentine* was an innovative work, which eschewed the annal-writing of the chroniclers and tried to fit historical events into some sort of theoretical framework. In 1521, Machiavelli published *The Art of War*, a work little admired by succeeding generations, since, as Anglo remarks, it had 'much more in common with antecedent military theory than with subsequent military practice'.[6] While working on the *Discourses*, he also wrote an unfinished epic poem, *L'Asino*, and a comic play called *La Mandragola*. The latter is taken seriously by some literary critics, though neither work adds anything to our understanding of Machiavelli's thought. They simply use verse and dramatic technique to highlight ideas developed in his political writings. Likewise, his treatises on war and history put forward no political opinions not to be found in *The Prince* and the *Discourses*. The entire political theory of Machiavelli is therefore contained in just two works – and not only the political theory, but also the philosophy (of man, of history) implicit in it.

Ever since the publication of *The Prince*, Machiavelli's legacy has provoked almost uninterrupted controversy. To this day, there is remarkably little consensus about what he actually said. The Machiavelli scholar confronts a bewildering labyrinth of contradictory interpretations and reactions that make one wonder if everyone is talking about the same person. Commentators seem to view the great Florentine through the prism of their own values and emotions. Bitter hatred and extravagant condemnation, on the one hand, have been met by unrestrained enthusiasm and lyrical praise, on the other. Initially, condemnation was very much in the ascendancy. *The Prince*, in particular, incurred the heartfelt wrath of the righteous, not to mention the simulated wrath of the hypocritical. In a climate of growing religious fervour, it was denounced as the Devil's catechism or the Ten Commandments reversed. One can scarcely exaggerate the violence done by Machiavelli's language and ideas to the discourse on virtues and vices that early modern Christians took for granted. *The Prince* advises rulers to employ deceit and cruelty; it advocates a form of politics in which conventional moral laws and standards of ethical conduct are merely snares for fools. To a society that regarded the relations between its parts as ruled by justice and equity and sanctified by religion, all this was more shocking than we can quite imagine. That politics could escape from the superintendence of Christianity, the strongest bond uniting men and nations, was (officially) unthinkable. Skulduggery and pagan debauchery were common enough *in practice*, and Catholic doctrine, as well as the new Protestant faith, allowed rulers to overstep the bounds of biblical morality in extreme situations. But Machiavelli was the first thinker to discuss political affairs without paying even ritual obeisance to the just, the noble and the sacred; the first thinker to elevate amoral pragmatism into a desirable principle. One of the early denunciations came from the pen of Cardinal Reginald Pole, who, in his *Apologia ad Carolum v. Caesarem*, assailed *The Prince* as a diabolical handbook for sinners. *All* of Machiavelli's works were condemned by the Roman Church and placed on the Index in 1559. But Catholics held no monopoly on the condemnation of Machiavelli. Protestant theologians, notably the French Huguenot Innocent Gentillet, were also shocked by his political cynicism and attacked him in print. The Machiavelli 'legend of hatred' was most developed in Elizabethan England, where the supposedly demonic character of his thought provided much fodder for poets and playwrights, who perhaps did more than politicians and theologians to propagate the Machiavelli myth.[7] References to the 'murderous Machiavel' were numerous in Elizabethan literature, and everywhere – most graphically in the plays of Shakespeare, Jonson and Marlowe – he was depicted as a professional inventor of stratagems and crooked tricks for rogues and gangsters. He was the great heavy of the Elizabethan theatre, embodying cunning and cruelty in equal measure.[8]

Not everyone, however, dismissed Machiavelli as an agent of the Evil One, and by the late eighteenth century a more favourable judgement had become popular. He came to be seen as a misunderstood lover of liberty and peace, whose *Prince* was designed to expose the wicked duplicity of tyrants. 'He professed to teach kings', Rousseau declared, 'but it was the people he really taught.'[9] Machiavelli, that is to say, was an unqualified republican who, under the guise of advising princes, tried to warn all free men of the dangers of despotism.

The growth of romantic nationalism added a new dimension to this counter-intuitive interpretation. Herder, the early prophet of German unity, claimed that *The Prince*, far from being an iniquitous guide for political criminals, was an objective study of sixteenth-century Italian politics by a patriot hoping to rescue his beleaguered country from an unholy alliance of foreign occupiers and indigenous collaborators. True, some of his counsels were shocking, but only strong medicine would suffice in the context. This view is not without plausibility. In an age of emerging nation-states, Machiavelli's Italy was not only subject to the whims of alien rulers, it was also divided into a number of mutually antagonistic jurisdictions. Moreover, the final chapter of *The Prince*, conveniently overlooked by those who stress the author's cynicism, urges Lorenzo, the Medici prince, to expel the 'barbarians' from Italian soil and 'lead Italy to her salvation'. Using passionate language similar to that of later Italian patriots, Machiavelli laments the desolate state of the country – 'lawless, crushed, despoiled, torn, overrun' – and demands a revival of the ancient Roman spirit.[10] These sentiments helped to inspire the nationalist movement known as the *Risorgimento* as Italy moved towards the liberation and unification of 1870. Machiavelli became a hero of Italian nationalism – an idealistic spokesman for the freedom of his country and the exemplar of all political virtues. The satanic villain was now a paragon of righteousness.

By the twentieth century, both the notion that Machiavelli was inspired by the Devil and the counter-notion that he was an idealistic republican patriot began to be questioned by those who saw him as a detached, dispassionate scientist, describing political behaviour as it actually was. Ernst Cassirer, for example, hailed him as the 'Galileo of politics', applying inductive methods to social and historical material.[11] An influential variation of this interpretation was put forward by Benedetto Croce, who argued that Machiavelli understood politics as pure power and technique – a utilitarian form of activity autonomous from conventional moral norms and governed by its own distinctive laws. The task of the political analyst, as the Florentine Secretary saw it, was to discover these laws, not to exorcize them or banish them from the world with 'holy water'.[12]

The Crocean idea that Machiavelli divorced politics from ethics was given an interesting twist by Charles S. Singleton, writing in 1953.[13] He argued that Machiavelli developed a conception of the state as a work of art; the great statesmen who have founded or maintained human associations are conceived as analogous to artists – moulders of men in the same way that sculptors are moulders of marble or clay. Politics thus leaves the realm of ethics and enters that of aesthetics. Machiavelli's originality, according to Singleton, consists in his view of political action as a form of what Aristotle called 'making' – the shaping of outward matter into a non-moral artefact, an object of beauty or use external to the creator (in this case a particular arrangement of human affairs) – and not of 'doing' (where Aristotle had placed it), action which defines the agent and therefore expresses the moral purpose of living a good life. Nevertheless, the role of Machiavelli the author is not that of *homo faber* but of *homo sciens*. The prince is an artist; Machiavelli himself is 'very much the experimental scientist, finding his laboratory either in the contemporary arena of political struggle or in history, ancient or recent'. Like a true scientist, 'he is interested in the particular instance only insofar as it may disclose a general principle'.[14] But in order to maintain his scientific perspective, Machiavelli must interpret political actions as artistic endeavours (efforts to impose one's will on external matter) and avoid all speculation about the moral good of the actors/artists or about their role in the drama of salvation.

The view of Machiavelli as a pure scientist was never universally shared. For Gramsci, the eminent Italian Marxist, he was the archetypal *politico in atto*, the active man of politics, embodying the unity of thought and action. Politics was, to him, a transforming, creative activity whose purpose was to mobilize the Italian 'nation' against the feudal aristocracy and papacy and their mercenaries. His 'prince' is therefore an anthropomorphic 'symbol' of a new and progressive 'collective will'. Gramsci compares Machiavellianism, as a political technique, to Marxism, since both take the 'essentially revolutionary' course of abandoning traditional ideological constraints in their efforts to change the world.[15] For other twentieth-century commentators, such as Herbert Butterfield, Machiavelli, while purporting to erect a science of statecraft, suffered from an equal lack of historical sense and empirical discipline. Obsessed by the heritage of ancient Rome, he deduced his political maxims in an a priori manner from classical theses concerning human nature or the historical process.[16] In a recent study, Maurizio Viroli portrays Machiavelli as 'a rhetorician', whose 'method of studying political reality was interpretative and historical rather than scientific', and who 'wrote to persuade, to delight, to move, to impel to act – hardly the goals of the scientist'.[17]

Meanwhile the older interpretations of Machiavelli refused to fade away. Viroli himself, following in the footsteps of Quentin Skinner and John Pocock, has vigorously defended the idea of Machiavelli as a freedom-loving republican, who saw politics not as a game of power and self-interest, but as 'the preservation of a community of men grounded upon justice and the common good'.[18] Or, as Skinner puts it, Machiavelli 'presents a wholehearted defence of traditional republican values'.[19] Foremost among these values, according to Pocock, was an Aristotelian conception of civic virtue, which assumed that man fulfilled his essential nature by 'acting upon his world' as a citizen, a participant with other citizens in decisions aimed at the distribution of a common good. Man, for Machiavelli, was a 'political animal', and the republic was 'the form in which human matter developed its proper virtue'.[20] This view of Machiavelli as a champion of liberty and self-governance is given a Marxist tinge by Benedetto Fontana's portrayal of him as the prototype of Gramsci's 'democratic philosopher', who 'teaches citizens to love one another' and seeks to overcome 'domination/subordination structures'. Machiavelli's goal, we are told, was a 'citizen democracy' where the people transform themselves into 'a self-determining subject' and where 'force and authority are no longer the ground of social and political life'.[21]

Interpreting Machiavelli as an idealistic spokesman for liberty and justice has become fashionable, but some commentators remain unconvinced. Harvey Mansfield, for example, derides such interpretations for their suggestion that 'Machiavelli was not Machiavellian', and reserves special contempt for the efforts by Skinner and Pocock to depict the Florentine as little more than an advocate of his native city's traditional republican values. Mansfield's Machiavelli was a bold innovator, a purveyor of 'immoralities and blasphemies', who did not see republicanism and tyranny as antonyms. Politics, as he understood it, was a struggle for domination, the purpose of which was 'to secure order rather than justice'. The Christians who denounced Machiavelli understood him only too well.[22]

Mansfield is a disciple of Leo Strauss, whose *Thoughts on Machiavelli*, published in 1958, delivered a stinging rebuke to all those who wanted to save 'Old Nick' from his sinister popular reputation – from modern echoes of the Elizabethan horror of a satanic Machiavelli. Adopting a neo-Elizabethan tone, Strauss professes himself a believer in 'the old-fashioned and simple opinion according to which Machiavelli was a teacher of evil'. As for his defenders, who offer the most ingenious excuses and reasons for his diabolical utterances, they have fallen victim to their idol's corrupting doctrine of moral relativism.[23] Mark Hulliung, while rejecting Strauss's investigative methods and naive moralism, also attacks attempts to rehabilitate Machiavelli 'as a sympathetic symbol in the mythology of liberalism and other humanistic creeds'.[24] He was not a good liberal or an incipient socialist; he was 'a pagan with a vengeance', the 'great subversive of the humanist tradition', who fashioned 'a transvaluation of values', in which 'what had been called virtue – Christian and Stoic virtue – is henceforth deemed corruption, and what had been considered vice – Machiavelli's politics – becomes virtue'. His was a moral code that exalted heroism and violence rather than the gentle virtues of enlightened professors.[25]

This violent disparity of judgements about Machiavelli's aims and achievements is superficially baffling and requires explanation. It should be noted, first of all, that Machiavelli was not a rigorous philosopher in the mould of, say, Hobbes or Locke. He did not develop a systematic or sophisticated account of political authority and obligation, neither did he show much interest in the analysis of political concepts. The quest for fine distinctions and abstract universals was alien to his type of mind, immersed as it was in the world of particulars. His concerns were more with the practical principles of statecraft. Viroli is right to say that Machiavelli's writings display the rhetorician's desire to persuade and arouse his audience. Like other Florentines of his social standing, Machiavelli was steeped in the rules of Roman rhetoric; vivid imagery and an insincere (sometimes ironic) invocation of values or prejudices dear to the listeners' or readers' hearts were familiar and accepted techniques. No one expected every statement to be a literal expression of the author's beliefs. Of course, there will always be a degree of doubt about the true intentions or opinions of a thinker who indulges in rhetorical ploys and flourishes. This may help to explain why Machiavelli presents so many faces to students of his ideas. Was he a malevolent counsellor of tyrants? Or a freedom-loving republican idealist? Was he an objective scientist? Or a passionate advocate of Italian unity? Was he a prophet of modernity? Or an antiquarian obsessed by ancient Rome?

These contrasting images of Machiavelli correspond, in part, to the apparently incompatible messages of his two major works. In *The Prince*, he advises rulers, good or bad, on how to 'seize absolute authority' and hold their fellow countrymen in thrall. The world of politics is depicted as a jungle in which there is no reality but power, and power is the reward of ruthlessness, ferocity and cunning. In such a jungle, the tyrant is king, and republican ideals – justice, liberty, equality – count for little. At best, they are pleasing fictions which can be used to disguise the exercise of naked power. As for the people, they are gullible and passive, though Machiavelli warns of the necessity to win their support and use them as a counterweight to the scheming and treacherous nobility.[26] *The Prince* is understandably seen as a vade-mecum for aspiring despots. The *Discourses*, on the other hand, is the work of a staunch republican and reminds us of Machiavelli's selfless devotion to the service of the Florentine republic. In this work, he advises both citizens and leaders of republics on how to preserve their liberty and avoid corruption. Self-government, he proclaims, is the surest guarantor of security and prosperity, since the interests of the many and those of a ruling prince are usually antithetical.[27] He adds that the people, as a collectivity, are more stable and exhibit

better judgement than most princes, and even likens 'the voice of a
people' to 'that of God'.[28]

At the very least, Machiavelli was sending confusing signals to his
readers. Historians have long discussed the relationship between his
two main works, their apparent inconsistency, and the extent to which
each represents his true thought. What is especially intriguing is that
the books were written at more or less the same time, making it unlikely that their author simply changed his mind. Exhaustive scholarship
has established that the first part of the *Discourses* was composed
in 1513. Machiavelli then interrupted this work to write *The Prince*
between July and December 1513. In 1515 he returned to the
Discourses, finishing it in 1517.[29] Some critics, recalling Machiavelli's
flawless republican credentials, have attributed *The Prince* to crass
opportunism. To be sure, in a famous letter of December 1513 to his
friend Francesco Vettori, Machiavelli revealed a wretched and abject
state of mind. Not only did he fear that the poverty caused by his
involuntary exile would reduce him to an object of contempt, he also
complained that his talents were going to waste. He made plain his
intention to dedicate *The Prince* to the Medici lords so that they might
employ him, 'even if they start by setting me to roll stones'.[30] This does
suggest that Machiavelli, like a good rhetorician (and a job-seeking
one at that), tailored his 'oration' to appeal to his audience – in this
case an authoritarian ruler. But it would be an oversimplification to
dismiss the work as an exercise in servile flattery. For a start, a true
courtier would have wrapped his advice up in soft words to make it
more palatable, as princes, no less than other men, like to think of
themselves as high-minded. In terms of the career he sought to revive,
The Prince is a self-defeating piece of work. Also, if we assume that
Machiavelli chose to play the Devil's advocate merely to gain employment, we will miss the powerful combination of logic and indignation
that generations of readers have found so compelling. He really did
believe that desperate times called for desperate measures. Outraged
by the foreign occupiers who threatened Florence and humiliated the
whole of Italy, he was willing to support *any* government that might
defend Florentine independence, get rid of the 'barbarians' and perhaps take the first steps towards the unification of Italy. The prospects
for a republican revival were, he realised, nil in the existing circumstances; it was therefore necessary to make the best of a bad situation.
Moreover, Machiavelli was committed – as we shall see – to a cyclical
theory of history, according to which a principate was a recurrent and

necessary phase in the life of states. All republics, he informs us in the *Discourses*, are founded by a single lawgiver, and all republics eventually sink into corruption. When they do, only tyrannical means can restore them to past glories.[31] While republics are to be preferred where possible, princely or despotic rule may be necessary when degeneracy and vice prevail. Let us also remember that Machiavelli's model for an ideal republic was ancient Rome, an expansionist and predatory state. Indeed, Butterfield argues that Machiavelli 'did not admire ancient Rome because the Romans had a republic; he admired republican government because it was the form under which ancient Rome had achieved unexampled greatness and power'.[32] The *Discourses* may be a republican text, but it does not equate republicanism with the reign of sweetness and light. Near the end of the work, for example, Machiavelli maintains that *any* action, however cruel or unjust, is legitimate if it helps to preserve the safety and independence of the country.[33] The Roman slogan, *salus populi suprema lex*, was his guiding principle. The 'contradictions' between *The Prince* and the *Discourses* are more apparent than real. The former, one might say, is the distilled essence of the latter. The mood and focus vary between one work and the other, but both show equally the basic values for which Machiavelli is notorious, such as the use of conventionally immoral means for political purposes and the belief that government depends on force and guile rather than universal standards of truth or goodness.

These considerations suggest a way of interpreting Machiavelli which allows us to avoid the simplistic dichotomies that bedevil the secondary literature. It is, after all, possible to be a republican without elevating republicanism into an absolute ideal. Likewise, passionate conviction is perfectly compatible with commitment to the empirical method. While we must of course resist the temptation to impose tidy formulas on a complex body of work, I shall argue that the key to understanding Machiavelli's thought (and legacy) lies in his dismissal of transcendence, or – to put it another way – his hostility to 'essentialism', to the positing of a priori goals, imposed on humanity by God or nature, and revealed to us by holy scripture or abstract reason. For Machiavelli, there were no unconditional values or norms, no universally valid modes of conduct, no supra-historical 'essences', distinct from the observable attributes and behaviour patterns of individuals. This immanentism, or worldly humanism, had two major implications, one methodological and the other substantive. First, it would seem to entail an empirical method of analysis. If the world does not form a rational structure, if there is no natural order of the soul, no hierarchy of ways of life or of goods, then the realm of the senses, practical reality, is the only source of knowledge. Neither introspection (turning inward in an examination of the self) nor deduction from first principles can help us to understand the world. Acknowledgement of this epistemological truth – if that is what it is – would not prevent us from forming particularistic attachments – to family, country, a certain code of values and so on – but it would encourage us to search for empirical explanations of those attachments, and of how we might preserve or enhance them. This is precisely what Machiavelli did. For him, the point of political analysis was to serve political ends, not to pile up information for its own sake.

The second implication of his worldly humanism was political realism. Machiavelli endeavoured to dispel illusions about political life, to unmask the myths of *both* reactionaries *and* utopian visionaries. It was his firm conviction that man was an inveterate spinner of fancies and delusive images, concealing the true nature of events. At bottom, politics was a clash of particular interests and particular 'utilities', a struggle for brute advantage, hidden by veils of euphemism. It follows that, to Machiavelli, republicanism was a practical preference, rooted in experience, not a universal truth, inherent in human nature or in God's plan for mankind. If circumstances dictated a deviation from the republican path, he would have no reason to oppose it. Believing as he did that there was no morality prior to society, he judged political arrangements solely in terms of their consequences.

Regarding anti-essentialism as the key to Machiavelli's thought can also help us to understand its historical significance. It will be my main theme, in what follows, that Machiavelli introduced a new way of conceiving politics. Classical and medieval thinkers always looked at political phenomena in the light of man's highest perfection, a transcendent standard by which to measure reality. Machiavelli, on the other hand, divorced politics from any kind of higher purpose, since he thought that all human purposes were grounded in practical reality. Thanks in no small part to his efforts, much modern political reflection has adopted an empirical perspective, disdaining speculation about imagined republics or perfect justice and focusing instead on real wants and needs. The aim is to relieve human suffering or to increase humanity's power over nature or to secure an orderly and prosperous existence.

My concluding chapter will show how this pragmatic approach to politics finds echoes all over the political spectrum. Marxists, starting with Marx himself, have always admired and, to a degree, imitated Machiavelli's efforts to demythologize politics, to reduce it to underlying power-relations.[34] But those associated with the right – the fascists, the classical elitists such as Mosca and Pareto – have sung his praises for the very same reason. It is clear, moreover, that what we might call 'sceptical liberalism' can also claim Machiavellian ancestry. For this tradition – carried forward by Hobbes and Hume and culminating in Bentham's coruscating attack on the nonsensical 'fallacies' of natural rights doctrine – politics, correctly understood, is not the collective implementation of abstract principles or timeless moral rules applicable to all forms of society; rather, it is merely a conflict of differing interests and goals and a consequent quest for the maximum satisfaction of human wants. Limited benevolence, as well as the varied and ephemeral circumstances of human life, mean that idealism must yield pride of place to social utility. Reason, in this tradition, is a purely calculating faculty rather than a source of objective moral truth. One of my contentions will be that Machiavelli anticipated later utilitarianism by suggesting – though not developing – a consequentialist understanding of morality.

This book will be critical of Machiavelli. It will explain why the relentless pursuit of power politics, at the expense of conventional moral rules, would be not just unacceptable but counter-productive in modern conditions. My final verdict, however, will be favourable. Machiavelli's rejection of transcendence, I will argue, offers two salutary lessons for modern politics and political philosophy: (1) that moral absolutism is often harmful and self-contradictory; and (2) that the primary goal of political life should be social equilibrium, not some preconceived idea of justice or human excellence.

But while his insights do transcend his historical context, Machiavelli was not of course speaking from the perspective of eternity. He was the product of a particular time and place. His fears and concerns were those of his contemporaries, and his mental horizons were limited by the commonplace assumptions of his society. Before we can assess the extent of his originality, or properly grasp the meaning or significance of his ideas, we must embark upon a detailed examination of the intellectual trends and social realities of Renaissance Italy.

2 • Setting the Context

Machiavelli is often seen as a typical man of the Renaissance – secular, sceptical, a worshipper of antiquity. But the meaning and significance of the Italian Renaissance have aroused considerable controversy. How far was this cultural movement original in its basic motifs? Most observers would agree that the Renaissance began during the mid-1300s (with the poems of Petrarch) and ended some time after the death of Raphael (1520) and before that of Tintoretto (1594). It was, according to Jacob Burckhardt's influential analysis, a distinctive period in human history, with sharp traits that constituted its particular Hegelian *Geist*.[1] The features singled out by Burckhardt and his many acolytes included rationalism, individualism and a keen appreciation of man's this-worldly capacities. Whereas the Middle Ages became a byword for barbarism and suffocating religiosity, the Renaissance was portrayed as a sudden and brilliant flowering of all kinds of spiritual activity. The traditional picture of the Middle Ages and the Renaissance was therefore one of antithesis between darkness and light.

Deepening knowledge of medieval life eventually challenged the conventional stereotypes. For example, historians discovered that the imitation of ancient models, supposedly the cause of cultural rebirth in the fourteenth and fifteenth centuries, was already a familiar theme in twelfth-century France, where the Chartres School promoted a revival of 'Latinity'. During this period, the teaching, writing and spoken use of Latin were qualitatively improved by the emergence of universities, an extension and amalgamation of cathedral schools and monastic training centres. The first university was founded in Paris (followed soon after by the founding of one in Oxford). The growing number of scholars and literates stimulated a love of letters and an eager cultivation of the Latin classics, expressed by a huge increase in the output of manuscripts from monastic scriptoria and secularized production centres. Moreover, the new universities of northern Europe provided a venue for the rediscovery of Aristotelian logic and its application to theological problems. Long before the Renaissance, Christian belief enjoyed a solid foundation of reason as well as faith.

Confronted by the evident refutation of medieval ignorance and obscurantism, some scholars went so far as to claim that the 'Renaissance' was only a later stage of a process begun much earlier, and that all the insights attributed to this supposedly golden age were prefigured in late medieval thought. The subtleties and details of this academic debate need not detain us.[2] Suffice it to acknowledge that history is indeed a continuous process; to divide it into distinctive phases is to impose artificial categories on an inherently shapeless flux of events and ideas. It would be absurd to seek for a temporal point at which the medieval era 'ends' and the Renaissance 'begins'. And yet we must, for the sake of giving coherence to our thoughts, still look for an *intellectual* line of demarcation between the two periods. Talking about the 'Renaissance' is not to foist an arbitrary scheme upon historical reality – one founded on a priori reasoning. All that is meant is that, in the interpretation of history, the infinitude of isolated facts must be arranged in some orderly pattern and so made accessible to historical analysis. 'Renaissance' and 'Middle Ages' are simply 'ideal-types' in the Weberian sense. Like all ideal-types, they are not faithful reflections of factual reality, but they do, through a process of abstraction, capture something 'essential' about that reality. As Marx reminded us, qualitative transformations can result from an accumulation of quantitative changes – that is to say, differences in degree become differences in kind. While there was no sudden intellectual upheaval, mid-fourteenth-century Italy did witness the emergence of a form of thought, known as 'humanism', that represented 'a fundamental change in man's outlook on life and the world'.[3] A brief exploration of this new paradigm, if you like, should help us to assess and appreciate Machiavelli's originality.

What were the humanists rebelling against? What was the medieval vision of the world? For a start, it was teleological. In order to understand a thing, we must – said the scholastic philosophers – go back to its first principle and show in what way it has evolved from this principle. The very first principle, the cause and origin of all things, is God, the 'unmoved mover' of the universe. He is the ultimate source of motion, being at rest himself. He transmits his force first to the things that are next to him, to the highest celestial entities. From here the force descends, by degrees, to our own world, the earth. But here we no longer find the same perfection. The higher world, the world of the celestial bodies, is made of an imperishable and incorruptible substance – the ether – and the movements of these bodies are eternal. In our own world, everything is liable to decay or deterioration. There is, it seems, a sharp discontinuity between the lower and higher worlds; they do not consist of the same substance and do not follow the same laws of motion. But the multiplicity of things is held together by a golden chain. All things whatsoever, whether spiritual or material, the choirs upon choirs of angels, humanity, organic nature, matter – all of them are bound in this golden chain about the feet of God. The essential unity of his creation, however, presupposes a strict hierarchy. The more remote a thing is from the prime mover, from the source of all being, so much the less is its grade of perfection or ethical value. The same principle was assumed to hold for the structures of political and social life. In the religious sphere, we find the ecclesiastical hierarchy that reaches from the pope, at the summit, to the cardinals, the archbishops, bishops, down to the lower echelons of the clergy. In the state, the highest power, derived from God, is concentrated in the emperor, who delegates this power to his inferiors, the princes, the dukes and all the other vassals. The feudal system is an exact image and counterpart of the general hierarchical system: it is an expression and a symbol of the universal cosmic order established by divine wisdom. One must therefore obey one's earthly rulers, though allegiance to God is primary; earthly life is nothing more than a preparation for entering the kingdom of heaven.

The universe was seen as a great allegory, an elaborate system of correspondences, where the different parts were related to one another not so much causally as symbolically. The prevailing world-view was, in sum, teleological (all creation is governed by divine purposes), holistic (everything is organically linked with everything else), hierarchical (both the cosmic and social orders are graded according to degrees of purity or proximity to God), static (God's plan, like God himself, is eternal and unchanging) and other-worldly (the human spirit is nourished by the inner life, whose centre lies outside the earthly city and carnal humanity). Inherent in this way of looking at reality was a denigration of all things political, for the essence of life was divorced from material and practical concerns. The ancient Greeks and Romans had understood 'the political' as a creative activity which transforms reality and enables man to fulfil his 'essential' nature. For the medieval Christians, by contrast, politics was the world of superficial appearances whose function was merely to curb the appetitive nature of 'fallen' man and ensure obedience to God's will. The prevailing ethos, by stressing the frailty of everything worldly, encouraged believers to accept their lot in life, to spurn earthly pursuits and instead seek the rewards of heaven through prayer and contemplation. The desire for secular honours or glory, reverence for one's homeland, enjoyment of the human body or the natural world – these were frowned upon as sinful distractions from the quest for eternal salvation. How and why did this mental framework change in the period of 'rebirth'?

At the risk of alienating scholars imbued with the traditions of Hegelian or Thomist idealism, we must accept that cultural transformations are bound up with attendant, if not antecedent, changes in economic and political institutions. We need not go to the Marxist extreme of reducing cultural phenomena to mere indices of alterations and readjustments of the social order. But in order to understand the gradual departure from medieval ways of thinking, it is necessary to examine the dynamic forces that were dissolving the medieval social structure, particularly in Italy, the 'cradle' of the Renaissance.

Medieval culture was predominantly feudal and ecclesiastical – the product of a society founded upon an agrarian, landholding economy. Italy, however, was atypical. Even in Roman times, the land had been densely populated, creating an urban life that the 'barbarian' invaders never wholly destroyed. 'Feudalism', as J. H. Plumb puts it, 'was planted in Italy but never rooted deeply there.'[4] The nucleus of social and political life was the town, not the castle. The presence of an urban proletariat, along with Italy's geographical position, making it the ideal trade-link between northern Europe and the sophisticated societies of the eastern Mediterranean, meant that commerce and industry could thrive as nowhere else. The social ideal of feudalism – an ordered, graded society, unchanging and unchangeable – was hopelessly anachronistic in a rapidly developing capitalist environment. By the beginning of the fourteenth century, Florence, in particular, exhibited all the traits of a bourgeois society: an economy characterized by risk and speculation, sharp fluctuations of wealth and income, a high degree of social mobility as well as flexibility of social intercourse, an open and tolerant cultural climate (heresy trials were rare) and a 'popular' government dominated by merchants, bankers and industrialists.[5]

Other factors combined to make the Italian situation unique. The Holy Roman Empire, whose writ theoretically extended to the city-states of northern Italy, found it impossible to control them from its seat beyond the Alps and ceased to have any real hold on Italian loyalties after the time of Dante (1265–1321). Even before then, the irrelevance of the residual rights of the emperor had caused the dominant ideological conflict of the Middle Ages between Papacy (supported by the Guelphs) and Empire (supported by the Ghibellines) to decline in significance. In other parts of Europe, contraction of the Empire's claims to sovereignty corresponded to the emergence of nation-states, impelled by the need to protect and regulate expanding markets. In Italy, however, centrifugal forces prevailed. The standard view, expressed by Machiavelli himself, is that the Papacy, which administered large parts of Italy and enjoyed a level of wealth that no king or emperor could match, used every ounce of its ingenuity and power to prevent the peninsula from becoming a unified nation-state. And yet, divisions within the Church, by undermining its spiritual and political authority, prevented it from exercising much influence in the north of Italy. The Papacy was transferred to Avignon in 1309, where it remained until 1378. From then until 1417, the Great Schism (between French and Italian factions) brought the ecclesiastical hierarchy into further disrepute.

With the disappearance of the Papacy and the Empire as effective political forces, much of Italy descended into a kind of anarchy. The power vacuum created by the decline of traditional authority allowed local powers to behave as they saw fit. In this atmosphere, the strong devoured the weak. From 1350 to 1450, Italy knew scarcely a month of peace, as the larger cities seized villages and lesser towns by force and provoked one another's enmity with predictable regularity. By the end of this period, though, the great city-states – Florence, Milan, Naples, Venice – had grown weary of endless strife. The emergent desire for more than a mere truce was recorded in the Peace of Lodi in 1454. None strong enough to dominate the others, the 'Italian Powers', the *Italiae potentiae* (as they called themselves), embarked on a precarious policy of equilibrium which lasted until 1494, when the French king invaded Italy and precipitated a series of armed conflicts more terrible than Italy had ever known.[6]

The Renaissance, then, was a time of pillage, rapine and turmoil. Italy became a playground for petty tyrants and oligarchs, rulers with questionable titles to legitimacy. In many cases, individuals with no dynastic claims were the driving force behind revolutions or coups, as the absence of an overarching order allowed particularism to flourish. Variety and instability of government, remodelling of the machinery of state, were nowhere so prevalent as in Italy. In this world of flux, political success depended on the exercise of superior shrewdness and ruthlessness, since power often had no foundation in tradition or

customary obligation. Even nominally republican states, such as
Florence, were controlled by powerful families or cliques who thought
nothing of unleashing aggression against their neighbours, or of conducting vicious feuds and vendettas against their domestic enemies.
This, paradoxically, was the backdrop for an unparalleled display of
cultural excellence. But diplomacy as we know it also arose in Renaissance Italy. By the fifteenth century, northern Italy displayed many of
the features of a miniature international system. The balance of power
created by the three great states of Milan, Venice and Florence caused
their leaders to work out the principles and the machinery of diplomatic practices which have governed international relations ever since.
One consequence of the Lodi Treaty was continuous consultation
among the signatories. From this emerged the permanent resident
ambassador, 'commonplace throughout Italy by 1460'.[7] Diplomacy, of
course, is all about forecasting the logic of events and devising effective responses. Those engaged in it become immersed in the mechanics
of power and perhaps lose sight of the purposes for which power is
supposedly exercised. There is a natural assumption that politics is an
end in itself, almost like a game of chess. This assumption was reinforced by the pervasive instability of the Italian scene, where rapid
changes in political fortune, brutal seizures of power, conspiracies and
aggression were the norm. Periods of peace had an air of imperman-
ency, as if war was the settled arrangement and its absence merely a
temporary deviation. An inevitable consequence was the general aban-
donment of the principle that government should be subordinated to
religious ends. Instead, the welfare of a particular prince or a particular state took priority. Almost a century before *The Prince* was written,
a tradition of 'realism' had developed in Italian political thinking. At
least on the practical level, issues of order and power were being confronted in almost strictly political terms. It was this secularization of
politics that emboldened more systematic thinkers, such as Leonardo
Bruni, to free themselves from the straitjacket of medieval political
thought and praise the ancient republican values of liberty and participation. It also made possible Machiavelli's experiment in 'pure' political theory, divested of religious imagery and religious values. By the
time Machiavelli wrote, the medieval view of the political realm as a
microcosm displaying the same structural principles of order prevalent
in creation as a whole had been shattered. Once seen as the embodiment of universal purposes, the political realm now stood exposed
as a battlefield where antagonistic forces struggled for supremacy.

Roman model. So successful were the humanists that imitation of antiquity became a fashion, extending even to leisure pursuits. Students would, on occasion, wear Roman dress and hold Roman feasts, and people would impress their friends and neighbours by tending their gardens according to classical principles gathered from Virgil and Horace.[10]

While it was by no means heretical or impious, humanism contained in its 'programme' some general ideas that threatened prevailing values. One of them was hostility to grand intellectual schemes which seek to organize and delimit every possibility within the pattern of a pre-established order. Implicitly challenging conventional religious cosmology, humanists preferred the conception of an open world, discontinuous and full of contradictions, infinitely various and immune to stultifying systematization. In place of a static world-view, they urged us to recognise 'the plastic mobility of all Being'.[11] Their rejection of a static reality, as presupposed by Scholastic and Aristotelian logic, gave them an empirical bent, which led them to criticize the medieval custom of treating texts as 'oracles from which one had to wrest the secret meaning'.[12] Texts, not factual reality, had become the object of knowledge, and empirical research, any attempt to place texts in *context*, was dismissed by hidebound cultural guardians as impertinence, or worse. To the medieval mind, the temporal dimension, the realm of particulars, was fleeting and impenetrable to human reason; the vocabulary of *telos* and final cause involved an ontology in which only unchanging, abstract universals were real and worthy of study. By paying attention to time and the existence of particulars, the humanists implied that change was real and that truth could evolve. This critical spirit – the tendency not simply to accept texts at their face value but to examine their provenance, credentials and contents with a wary eye – obviously posed a threat to medieval certainties.

Even more subversive was the humanist emphasis on man as the moulder and maker of himself and his world.[13] For example, adjectives such as 'divine' and 'heroic' were increasingly used to describe painters, princes and other mere mortals.[14] There developed a new sense of the human being as agent – as someone responsible for his actions, as the fundamental building block of human society. During the Middle Ages, as Burckhardt observed, man was 'conscious of himself only as a member of a race, people, party, family, or corporation – only through some general category'. Renaissance Italians instead developed a heightened awareness of the separateness of self from the rest of reality. Consciously dividing experience into subjective and objective components, they came to value singularity, or individuality, to appreciate their own autonomy, which – in the medieval world – had been hidden beneath 'a common veil . . . woven of faith, illusion, and childish prepossession'.[15] The stress on human agency was especially visible in humanist historical writings. Whereas medieval historians typically interpreted events in moral and providential terms, regarding success and failure as divine rewards for virtue or divine punishments for sin, humanist historians secularized the interpretation of history, viewing earthly affairs as the outcome of *human* aims, skills and resources.[16] Rather than being helpless counters in God's unfolding plan, humankind were themselves the authors of their own fortune and misfortune. Nothing was preordained. Moreover, if historical events could to some degree be controlled through intelligent political action, then the historical record could provide models for emulation and a framework by which human actions could be comprehended and judged. By the fifteenth century (*il quattrocento*), the appeal to historical example as justification for a particular policy or viewpoint – a method we associate with Machiavelli – had become a standard technique of Florentine political discourse.

The emphasis on man, on his dignity and privileged place in the universe, engendered a desire, as Burckhardt put it, 'accurately to describe man as shown in history, according to his inward and outward characteristics'.[18] The exploration of the individual personality, of the uniqueness of one's feelings, opinions and experiences, was a feature of the descriptive literature of the time and also informed the new art of comparative biography, which was based on the assumption that the distinctive traits of remarkable men could be isolated and imitated.[19]

The preoccupation with individual subjectivity had its most revolutionary consequences in the plastic arts. In medieval times, as we have seen, identity was determined by group membership. To describe an individual was therefore to specify an exemplar of the group to which he belonged. His personal characteristics, those that might distinguish him from the rest of the group, were relegated to the realm of irrelevant particulars. Since medieval artists were concerned with prototypes, not individuals, they did not need to portray realistic figures in convincing space. The primitive visual technology which makes medieval art seem so artificial to our eyes was well-suited to their abstract purpose: the symbolic expression of religious ideas. Truth to nature, even if it were technically possible to achieve, would have detracted from the stark simplicity of the message. But the Renaissance, being fascinated with the individual human being, as opposed to the archetype or mere category, revived the classical anxiety to represent the human body accurately, to show emotions not symbolically but as they are actually seen on human faces, and to depict the infinite physical variations that distinguish human beings from one another. Renaissance artists wanted to create realistic human beings in realistic settings. Naturalism, the accurate representation of reality, became a prime artistic objective. But this did not involve simply the faithful copying of nature, the creation of a mirror image of the physical universe. Instead, Renaissance artists selected particular elements of the visible world and organized them rationally and scientifically to create an *illusion* of reality. For example, the *content* of a painting might include a surreal juxtaposition of Christian and pagan imagery, but the *style* would always be naturalistic. In pursuit of their aims, artists (especially sculptors) intensively studied the physical remnants of classical antiquity – Roman statues, or at least pieces of them, that had survived the ravages of time. For painting, however, the crucial breakthrough was made by Filippo Brunelleschi with his invention of perspective, the geometric device that allows an artist to create the illusion of three-dimensional space upon a flat surface. With mathematical accuracy objects could be fixed and their relations to one another established in this three-dimensional world. The natural effect was also enhanced by the technique of foreshortening, or representing a figure as shorter than its actual height and adjusting its proportions in order to give an illusion of recession or projection. The application of scientific principles to visual presentation freed painters, in particular, to treat subjects in a more adventurous and imaginative way than in the past. An impression of motion could be conveyed, figures could come alive and be placed in complex settings. Even the appreciation of the artistic object became more dynamic. The physical depth afforded by perspective encourages the onlooker to step into the scene, so to speak, and directly experience the emotions depicted in the painting.[20]

The artistic achievements of the Italian Renaissance were spectacular. Donatello, Michelangelo, Leonardo da Vinci, Raphael – these geniuses were only the tip of a very large iceberg. And their greatness was made possible by two powerful currents within the humanist perspective. The first was rationalism – using the higher spiritual faculties to discover the guiding principles of the world and to represent them in word and form. Renaissance artists conceived of space and the physical universe as phenomena which could be defined, measured and not philosophy. The gist of his argument was that the human intellect, though not material in its substance, was capable of attaining knowledge only of corporeal objects. By maintaining that all our knowledge derives from sense perception, Pompanazzi demolished the ideal of contemplation which finds its necessary fulfilment in a higher world beyond the grave. He substitutes for it the ideal of a moral virtue which – unlike communion with the infinite – can be attained during the present life. The argument was Aristotelian in form (though Aristotle himself asserted that the primary aim of human life must be found in contemplation). The speculative intellect, Pompanazzi claims, is not characteristic of man as man, but belongs properly to God. Although all men have something of it, very few, if any, possess it fully or perfectly. On the other hand, the practical intellect truly belongs to man, for every normal human being can attain it perfectly by leading a blameless life of moral virtue. Thus man's present, earthly existence is credited with a significance that does not depend on any hopes or fears for the future.[22]

Pompanazzi was far from being the only Italian thinker to enlist Aristotle's support for a life of social duty and endeavour. In the early Quattrocento, a doctrine now dubbed 'civic humanism' was developed by Leonardo Bruni, Chancellor of the Florentine republic as well as a famous humanist. He and his supporters adopted the Aristotelian view that man was a civic or political animal, that the individual fulfilled his nature and attained virtue (his highest perfection) only by participating with other citizens in pursuit of the common good. On this interpretation, the classical insistence on civic virtue and communal well-being was completely in harmony with Christian morality.[23] And the humanists practised what they preached. Like Bruni, many of them were men of affairs: lawyers and public administrators, diplomats, secretaries of cities and advisers of princes. Partly under their influence, the crippling weight of renunciation which had officially lain on civil consciences for a millennium was gradually being lifted. By the mid-fifteenth century, the magistrate, the soldier, the businessman could hold up his head. Even artists, who were largely anonymous during the Middle Ages, became celebrities, commanding admiration and honours, not to mention large fees. The growth of individualism, the desire to be different from one's neighbours, expressed itself in the pursuit of riches and fame. Wealth, explicitly condemned in the Bible and the cause of many a guilty conscience, came to be seen as a source of personal and public happiness. Princes and rich men enhanced their images by financing paintings and statues, erecting and decorating buildings, and possessing fine houses adorned by beautiful books and furniture. Few expected such people to live lives of Christian abnegation, or to fret, as Dante did, about the spiritual emptiness of fame and fortune.

Still, while wealth could bring you prestige and even veneration in Renaissance Italy, it never completely lost its association with impiety and guilt. Rich patrons were often trying to atone for their suspect profits. Moneylenders were especially conscious of their moral debt to the community. Fundamental to any banking business is the receiving of interest on loans. In the Middle Ages, this was considered to be usury, a sin condemned by the Bible. The survival of this prejudice well into the fifteenth century was a serious disability to the banking business. Yet it was of fundamental importance to art patronage, for the accepted way of expiating the sin of usury was to finance the repair, construction or decoration of some religious foundation. This may help to explain why the Medici, the most successful bankers in Florence, felt obliged to devote a large proportion of their profits to such ends. Perhaps the greatest of all patrons was Cosimo de' Medici (1389–1464), who dominated Florentine public life for an entire generation, using his money to renovate monasteries, to build palaces and chapels, to provide commissions for all the leading artists, from Donatello down, and to employ dozens of professional scribes in copying classics for his library. In their readiness to promote culture, the rich and powerful were motivated not just by religious scruples but by political expediency as well. The very competitiveness of Italy's independent statelets encouraged rulers – many of them lacking in historical or constitutional legitimacy – to bolster their power with the embellishments of scholarship and art. For the Renaissance, as Paul Johnson points out, 'was one of the few times in human history when success in the world's game – the struggle for military supremacy and political dominion – was judged at least in part on cultural performance'.[24] Haunted by the insecurity of politics, rulers found it opportune to conform to the ideal of the *uomo universale*, the man who has cultivated all sides of his personality.

Although humanism was neither a philosophy in the technical sense nor a systematic, self-conscious ideology in the manner of, say, Marxism, it nevertheless represented a new and distinctive outlook. What the humanists provided was an unmistakable, if generally implied, critique of the culture and social values of medieval Christendom, based on their reverence for classical antiquity. In their view, the failings of modern Christian life could mostly be traced to the loss of the classical heritage: the practical wisdom and military power of ancient Italy. As one commentator remarks, 'to celebrate the past was inevitably to criticise the present'.[25] The condemnation of pride and vainglory, for example, had been central to Christian teaching since its beginnings, but humanists saw that reviving ancient traditions of public virtue would be impossible if princes and citizens were not encouraged to attain fame and adulation. The idea of *libido dominandi* (lust for power) was prevalent in Italian Renaissance thinking, as was praise for heroic actions.[26] Indeed, self-assertion words abound in the literature of the period – *gloria, onore, valore, concorrenza* (competition).[27] Although the humanists posed no direct threat to the ecclesiastical polity of the Church, they articulated a new, lay view of Christian society that fused established Christian values with ancient pagan ones. To a large extent, they were making a virtue of necessity. Renaissance princes were already behaving as if the medieval subordination of political to religious ends was a hopeless anachronism. The *libido dominandi* was an omnipresent reality, while the orthodox Christian injunction to avoid the temptations of wealth and glory became little more than a fig-leaf for society's 'losers'. Given the fluctuating distribution of power between (and within) city-states, people became acutely aware that the political system was not a gift from God but a human artefact. The belief that force was the real key to understanding politics gained currency among the Florentine ruling elite; and, by the time Machiavelli put pen to paper, it was almost universally accepted.[28] One of his diplomatic colleagues, Francesco Guicciardini, formulated the point in his inimitably succinct way: 'State authority is nothing but violence over subjects.'[29] By the end of the fifteenth century the idea of an immovable God-given order had been overcome by a more dynamic vision of a world in evolution, in flux, where God (and the Devil) no longer pulled the strings.

3 • Hostility to Metaphysics

It was the effective disintegration of the medieval conception of political life that allowed Machiavelli to develop his distinctive views. One isolated thinker, no matter how great, can hardly change reality in any fundamental way. What he *can* do is to reinforce emergent trends or patterns of behaviour by codifying, or giving theoretical shape, to them. Politics as a clash of opposing forces was the reality Machiavelli encountered; he did not invent it. Nor was he the first person in early modern Italy to admire antiquity and worldly values – a common enough attitude amongst the humanists who preceded him. These environmental influences and intellectual debts induce some commentators to interpret his texts strictly in terms of their context. Allan Gilbert, for example, has argued that *The Prince* was fairly commonplace, being similar in both content and style to treatises written in the familiar genre of advice-books for monarchs, a literary form originating in the Middle Ages but still popular during the Renaissance.[1]

It is true that the *form* of *The Prince* – its logical structure, even the Latin chapter-headings – conforms to traditional rhetorical formulae and practices. But it never seems to occur to Gilbert that Machiavelli may have used an established Christian genre for purposes of subversion. After all, unconventional messages are especially striking if they are presented in a conventional manner. An erotic drawing in a prayer-book is likely to make a greater impression than an identical drawing in a pornographic magazine. The danger of contextual analysis, of course, is that a thinker's originality could somehow get lost in the relentless hunt for precursors. What is needed is a detailed examination of the ways in which Machiavelli's ideas *departed from* the traditional 'mirror-of-princes' literature. Another Gilbert, Felix, undertook precisely this task in a renowned article published a year after his namesake's contribution.[2]

The medieval approach to the genre, he maintains, was typified by Egidio Colonna, one of the most influential Aristotelians of the late thirteenth century, who argued purely deductively from general propositions and assumptions regarding the nature of the universe. In his way of thinking, the whole of man's earthly existence is coordinated with the life beyond. From this premise, he deduces the prince's place in the world. The prince is the intermediary between God and man, and attributes of rulership must flow from this proposition. Princes, for instance, should not aim to acquire honour, power or wealth; instead, they should set an example to their subjects by following the principles of natural justice.[3] At first glance, says Gilbert, the humanists seem to have nothing in common with Colonna. While for Egidio the good ruler's reward was a sublime position in the next world, for the humanists his reward was fame. Furthermore, the humanists introduced a new methodology. For the most part, they supported their arguments with historical examples and eschewed abstract theoretical speculation. The examples, needless to say, were taken exclusively from antiquity, particularly ancient Rome. Yet, Gilbert continues, careful study of humanist writings on the prince 'will reveal a number of traits which they have in common with the medieval conception'. Like the medieval authors, the humanists attempted to describe the *ideal* prince. In both cases, the qualities of this model sovereign were determined by unrealistic political assumptions. The tasks of the Quattrocento prince were confined, like those of his medieval counterpart, to the administration of innate justice and the maintenance of peace. Consequently, the just and humane king or prince remained the ideal.[4] But, as suggested above, in the humanist catalogue of princely attributes, purely worldly ones, such as *magnificentia* and *majestas*, took their place beside the religious ones. The former type, moreover, were considered from the point of view of their empirical effects, their advantages and disadvantages being weighed. *Liberalitas*, say, was regarded not so much as a good in itself but as a means of consolidating the power of the ruler. Patrizi (1412–94) and Pontano (1426–1503) even began to raise the question of whether princely virtues might be in some respects different from those of private citizens, but they did not take it seriously enough to supply a systematic answer or to work out a consistent doctrine of political necessity. Although they had glimpses of a unique political morality, Machiavelli's humanist predecessors 'invariably started by accepting the traditional identity between the ideal prince and the ideal human being'. There is no real appreciation of the power struggles and egoistic purposes which dominate political life. The Quattrocento princeship literature remained enclosed within the Christian framework, where man's ultimate purpose is to attain a state of grace, and where the rational course of action is always the moral one, dictated by natural law.[5]

Machiavelli did indeed adapt the logical structure of *The Prince* to the conventional literary form of the advice-book genre, but he removed all traces of the idealized human personality from his portrait of the prince. Conventional Christian concerns yielded to reasons of state. Machiavelli's deviance is nicely illustrated by his redefinition of the pivotal concept of *virtù*. For the humanists, *virtù* was essentially equivalent to 'virtue' as we understand it – a moral good, indicating a humane, prudent, wise form of behaviour. For Machiavelli, *virtù* was more like a force of nature, including in its meaning such things as 'ambition', 'drive', 'courage', 'energy', 'will-power' and 'shrewdness'. While he agreed with the humanists that the prince must personify *virtù* he did not see *virtù* and lack of scruple as in any way contradictory. He removed the word's Christian associations.[6] In fact, the Latin cognate, *virtus* (with its connotations of patriotism, manliness and courage), resembles *virtù* in the special Machiavellian sense. By divorcing the prince's *virtù* from the conventional catalogue of Christian virtues, Machiavelli constrained the ruler's behaviour only by political necessity. His subversion is also evident in his use of the historical method. Like the humanists, his aim was to apply classical wisdom to the problems of his own time. It was an axiom of Renaissance thinking that the study of classical antiquity held lessons for the modern world, and that ancient Rome had a unique exemplary status. But humanists were certain that Roman texts, in particular, embodied prudential *and* ethical principles of eternal value. The idea was to extract exempla of good and evil, effective and ineffective conduct. Machiavelli, on the other hand, wanted to draw only pragmatic, not distinctively moral, lessons from the ancient past. If he was willing to countenance cruelty, fraud and deceit, it was because he saw politics as a form of activity unconditioned by any assumptions or aims of a Christian character. This did indeed represent a decisive break with tradition. Time and again, medieval philosophers had quoted the saying of St Paul that all power derives from God. The rights and duties of both rulers and subjects are grounded in the intentions of God and the limitations of human reason as created by God. Humanist thinkers before Machiavelli at least paid lip-service to the divine origin of the state, but he disdained to make even that concession. What Copernicus, his contemporary, achieved in the realm of cosmology, Machiavelli achieved in the sphere of politics. The Polish astronomer replaced the Aristotelian cosmological system – the conventional orthodoxy – with a new system where we no longer find a division between the 'higher' and 'lower' worlds. All movements whatever, the movements of earth and those of celestial bodies, obey the same universal rules. For Machiavelli, too, there are no privileged points in the universe, no 'above' and 'below'. The same principles and natural laws hold in the physical and political orders alike. It is often remarked that he employs phrases and analogies of a positively naturalistic or medical character. References to 'natural necessity' and 'natural' desires or difficulties occur frequently in his analyses of political forces.[7] In order to describe the state, he is forever racking his brains for expressions which compare it to a plant, roots and all,[8] and for similes in which its development is likened to the development of a human body – so much so that he came to adopt a naturalistic view of the state itself, attributing to it the qualities of a natural phenomenon: birth, growth, decline and death.[9] There may be a contradiction between this deterministic naturalism and Machiavelli's insistence that a virtuoso politician can decisively shape events. But perhaps not, since Machiavelli sees the politician as a sort of doctor, who uses his skill to expel bad 'humours' from the body politic and restore it to health, though it is still destined – like the human body – to decay and perish.[10]

Machiavelli's many references to nature carry no teleological baggage, no suggestion of an immanent purpose or design. The nature of man is for him an empirical question. When previous political philosophers, humanist and medieval alike, undertook to define human nature, they did not purport to tell us how man actually behaves, but rather what his end or destiny is, what he is created for. Some contextual historians, in a manner reminiscent of (Allan) Gilbert, tend to gloss over this distinction between Machiavelli and his predecessors, subsuming his thought into the tradition of Aristotelian republicanism that dominated Florentine political science during the Quattrocento.[11] The republicans, or 'civic humanists', borrowed a teleological view of virtue from Aristotle, insisting that man is by nature a political animal, who achieves fulfilment through activity devoted to the common good. The city is founded on friendship, according to the conventions of civic humanism; on doing and sharing things in common, not upon the mere exchange of commodities or reciprocal protection. Purveyors of this philosophy, in Pocock's words, 'depicted human social life as a universality of participation' where particular men 'met in citizenship to pursue and enjoy the universal value of acting for the common good'. In this 'perfect partnership of all citizens', only 'the political animal could be a truly good man'.[12] By deploying this 'paradigmatic

structure' in their interpretation of Machiavelli, the contextual historians do not intend to deny his originality, but they certainly minimize
it, claiming, in the case of Pocock, that his thought functions 'within
humanist, Aristotelian, and medieval limits'.[13] Skinner is even more
forthright in affirming the Florentine's conventional republicanism
when he informs us that 'Machiavelli not only presents a wholehearted
defence of traditional republican values; he also presents his defence in
a wholeheartedly traditional way'.[14]

Can this be so? While Machiavelli was sympathetic to republicanism, he barely mentioned Aristotle and never defined politics in
transformative or 'expressive' terms. As for a city based on friendship,
Machiavelli explicitly rejected this as utopian. Those who picture a
united commonwealth, without dissension or 'Unkindness betwixt
Men', are 'egregiously mistaken', he tells us.[15] Unless we start out
with the assumption that all thinkers are trapped in their historical
and intellectual context, it is hard to escape the conclusion that the
Aristotelian mode of analysis was completely alien to Machiavelli.
Nowhere does he talk about man having a spiritual purpose which is
not simply derivable from a description of his observable behaviour.
In medieval times, this idea was used to justify the authority of
Church and state, as well as the passivity of the masses, for whom God
had prescribed a life of obedience and denial. Although the humanists
rejected the medieval denigration of the earthly city, they retained the
Aristotelian teleology and even the deductive methods of the theologians. They put the same questions: 'What is the essential nature of
man?' 'What are God's plans for him?' There is the same preoccupation with definitions and the same belief that moral truths can be
derived from them. Most humanists who reflected on man and society
were too pious to adopt a wholly empirical perspective on reality. Man
for them formed part of a universe in which were displayed greater-
than-human purposes.

By contrast, the only purposes that Machiavelli recognizes are man's
own purposes; and all political arrangements are, in his eyes, human
contrivances for human ends. As we shall see more clearly in a later
chapter, Machiavelli thinks that psychologically man is a mass of insatiable desires.[16] While not necessarily disagreeing with this as an
explanation of why man behaves as he does, Christian and Aristotelian
philosophers would have considered such behaviour to be a deviation
from the natural and the good. The proper function of the political
unit is therefore to allow man to achieve his full potential as a moral

being by creating the type of environment where human excellence can thrive. But Machiavelli has no notion of man becoming actually what he is potentially. Human nature is not something that must be 'realized'; it is determined by actual characteristics. Men are political animals only in the sense that they must concern themselves with one another as *means* to the satisfaction of their desires. Glory, to take one example, cannot be attained in the absence of public recognition. Likewise, access to scarce material goods requires power over others, or else the ability to manipulate their thought processes. Although Machiavelli refers to the 'common good' as the end of the state,[17] he has in mind not so much a moral end as the survival, security and happiness of the citizenry. He was not so naive as to believe that the inhabitants of his beloved Roman republic acted for the common good. To the contrary, they sought their 'own utility', often at the expense of others. What saved them from social dissolution was not a mass spirit of altruism but a common 'love of the fatherland', which encouraged a practical willingness to compromise, where necessary.[18]

For Machiavelli, the universe is not governed by Reason or Mind; the structure of reality is basically a meaningless system of physical motions. The only natural laws he mentions are laws of physical necessity. He makes no reference to any ideal order, to any doctrine of man's place in the great chain of being, to any far-off event towards which creation moves. He has no notion of human development or progress in pursuit of ends ordained by God or by nature. Even his theory of cyclical recurrences and repetitions in history, Berlin notes, 'is not metaphysically guaranteed'.[19] Rather, such *corsi* and *ricorsi* occur 'by chance'. Although cyclical changes are necessary and follow an unalterable sequence (they are not random), they have not been planned by any being, nor do they serve any fixed design. In using the word 'chance', Machiavelli wants to say that these cycles take place because of the natural inclinations of men in groups and not because of any 'essence', or 'final cause', governing human society or human individuals.[20] According to Berlin, the originality of Machiavelli's viewpoint can hardly be exaggerated. For one of the deepest assumptions of western political thought, scarcely questioned before Machiavelli, is the doctrine 'that there exists some single principle which not only regulates the course of the sun and the stars, but prescribes their proper behaviour to all animate creatures'. Central to this doctrine 'is the vision of an impersonal Nature or Reason or cosmic purpose, or of a divine Creator whose power has endowed all things and creatures or inscribed in human nature (as the Aristotelians say). 'Good' behaviour is simply behaviour that enjoys approbation because long experience teaches us that its effects are usually beneficial; 'bad' behaviour, conversely, is simply behaviour that invites disapprobation because equally long experience teaches us that its effects are usually harmful. Likewise, 'justice' stems from man's fear of suffering evil at the hands of others; the concept refers to a set of rules and principles that evolve to deal with this concern, and there is no reason why they should not differ, in content if not in form, from one civilization to another.[23] This is why, for Machiavelli, law is an 'external' thing; it is not handed down by God to the mortals made in his immortal image, nor does it derive from moral purposes that are inherent in human nature. Law is nothing but a form of command, rooted in superior force or superior craft.

Though amply supported by textual evidence, this 'secular' interpretation of Machiavelli is not universally accepted. There *are* commentators – a small minority, to be sure – who view him as a sincere, if iconoclastic, Catholic, blessed with a profound sense of the eternal and determined to maintain the link between politics and religion. A classic statement of this interpretation was made, some years ago, by Felice Alderisio. What *his* Machiavelli admired about the ancient Romans was not their paganism but their 'fear of divinity', along with their ability to combine piety with martial and civic virtues.[24] Those who deny that Machiavelli possessed a 'resolute and lofty Christian consciousness' perpetuate 'a vulgar legend'.[25] True, he wanted to combat the 'deformations' of Catholic dogma, especially its 'fanatical disavowal' of earthly things and its indifference to the common good. Much like later reformers, he urged a 'more vigorous, more ample, more humane, and more elevated interpretation' of Christianity, one that could rescue the Church from its doctrinal distortions, on the one hand, and its secular corruption, on the other. So far from rejecting the primacy of religion, he regarded it as 'the immanent and transcendent end' of the state. Our purpose on earth is to carry out 'the divine plan', and this requires 'active participation' in social life, the accomplishment of mundane tasks assigned by God.[26] If Alderisio is right, Machiavelli would not have felt embarrassed in the company of that other (and somewhat younger) scourge of ecclesiastical misdeeds, Martin Luther.

This 'Christian' interpretation of Machiavelli seemed to become moribund until it was revived in 1989 by Sebastian De Grazia. *The Prince*, he informs us, comprises 'significant metaphysical and theological statements'.[27] As for the *Discourses*, it is 'a fundamental work moral influence it exerts is, for Machiavelli, that of a coercive force, proceeding from above, subjecting human minds to a firm discipline and assisting in the fulfilment of civic obligations. There is no need for religion to rest on truth, provided that it is socially effective.[35] Religion is thus deprived of its mystical and spiritual content; it is nothing more than a useful fiction, a tissue of myths, whose worth depends entirely on its capacity to promote solidarity and cohesion.

So his hostility to the Papacy, his desire to see the Church of Rome reformed, was prompted by motives quite different from those that inspired the dissenters and reformers of the time. The Catholic Church, in Machiavelli's opinion, was to be condemned for its *practical* failings, not because it had strayed from the path of true righteousness. First of all, its transparently hypocritical commitment to financial accumulation and territorial aggrandizement had caused Italians to lose 'all devotion and all religion – which brings with it infinite inconveniences and infinite disorders'. Furthermore, the Papacy had kept Italy divided. For it was too weak to unite the entire peninsula, yet strong enough to prevent others from doing so, 'for fear of losing dominion over its temporal things'.[36] But he was not just opposed to the corrupt antics of the Papacy; he also attacked Christianity as such and contrasted its degenerate values with the noble values enshrined by pagan religion. As if anticipating Nietzsche, he levelled at Christianity the now familiar reproach of having made men humble, unmanly and feeble. Christian dogma stressed the frailty of everything worldly and urged the faithful to cultivate the inner life, to search for individual salvation in eternity. Pride was frowned upon as the root of all evil. But, in a predatory world, what society could flourish or even persist if all its citizens displayed the traditional Christian virtues of humility and passivity? If good men pursue an other-worldly image of human excellence, they will surely fall prey to 'criminal men'. Meekness is an invitation to others to be unjust and therefore a bad quality in a citizen. The Roman version of piety, on the other hand, encouraged men to have a proper sense of their own dignity, to avenge an insult or an injury, to protect their families, their neighbours and the integrity of their community. Another point in favour of Roman religion, according to Machiavelli, was that it imposed little in the way of doctrine; it consisted mainly of ceremony and ritual, whose effect was to strengthen social ties. A dogmatic religion like Christianity could have the opposite effect. Personal adherence to certain doctrines creates the possibility of conflict with the community and absorbs spiritual energies which might otherwise be devoted to it. He felt sympathy for the man of principle, capable of self-sacrifice, but not for the man of conscience, torn between public duty and private conscience. With romantic longing, he gazed towards the strength, grandeur and beauty of life in antiquity, and towards the principles of its *mondana gloria*. Machiavelli promoted the ideal of a 'new man', in whom grandeur of spirit (*grandezza dell'animo*) and strength of body (*fortezza del corpo*) combined to create heroism. Betraying not the slightest sign of reluctance or compunction, the Florentine broke with the spiritualizing ethic of Christianity, which deprecated the natural impulses of the senses. It is true that he regarded this as a 'false' understanding of Christ's message, and that he denounced those who had 'interpreted our religion according to idleness [*ozio*] and not according to virtue [*virtù*]'.[37] The fact remains, however, that Machiavelli valued 'our religion' only for its instrumental qualities, such as they were. His commitment to Christianity was cultural rather than doctrinal or emotional.

The Christian psychology of sin and redemption is nowhere to be found in his two major works. The idea of sin in Machiavelli has nothing in common with the idea of sin as breaking a commandment of God. Instead, 'sins' are political errors, often committed by rulers who try to obey Christian ethics when objective circumstances require mercilessness or deception.[38] The anguished conscience, seeking atonement or comfort, has no place in his cosmology. The Christian virtues he decries – self-abnegation, humility and other-worldliness – are precisely those virtues connected with the interior good of the soul as it struggles against our 'evil' impulses. Indeed, the word 'soul' (*anima*) is conspicuous by its absence from *The Prince* and the *Discourses*. As conceived by Plato and Aristotle, and later in Christian theology, the soul differentiates man from the rest of nature, giving him a special dignity. Whereas *anima* never occurs in Machiavelli's two main works, *animo* ('spirit' or 'spiritedness') occurs frequently and is used in the sense of 'fighting spirit', or the will to defend one's own (body, family, homeland and so on) against actual or potential enemies. Spirit, thus construed, depends on physicality, whereas 'soul' (*anima*) always transcends physicality. Again, Machiavelli seems to be saying that we are primarily objects in nature, and that we are therefore governed by 'natural necessity'.[39]

Neither do we find in Machiavelli the usual Christian imagery of divine and diabolic intervention in earthly affairs. He never invoked a supernatural will to explain the ultimate reason for things. A brief excursion here into Machiavelli's discussion of 'fortune' would help to illustrate this point. The classic expression of the role that fortune had in the medieval system is to be found in a famous passage of Dante's *Inferno*.[40] Men, we learn, are in the habit of speaking of fortune as if she were an irrational and independent being. But such a conception is the result of human blindness. Whatever fortune does, she does not in her own name but in that of a higher power. She is an *ancilla dei*, an agent of divine providence. She may be pitiless and indiscriminate in her bestowal of gifts, but her very indifference to human merit in the disposition of her rewards serves to remind us that the goods of this life are unworthy of our pursuit, that the quest for worldly riches and glory is of no account in the final scheme of things, and that we must therefore free ourselves from such unworthy distractions in order to seek our heavenly home. The Christian element is removed in Machiavelli's description. He revives the pagan notion of fortune as an essentially uncontrollable goddess who may nevertheless grant her favours to a man of *virtù* (*virtus* in Latin), a man of courage and audacity.[41] Where such *virtù* is lacking, fortune will be pitiless, making or breaking men with wilful abandon. Yet, when Machiavelli personifies fortune as a fierce goddess, he appears to be speaking metaphorically. Fortune, in his writings, is not so much a supernatural figure as a literary or rhetorical device to describe the logic of events, the external constraints on human behaviour, the web of earthly accidents in their inexorable succession. Machiavelli's expressed desire to avoid 'superfluous decoration' in his prose style never deterred him from employing figurative language.[42] In *The Prince*, he also compares fortune to an elemental force – a raging river, which can be controlled by 'constructing dykes and embankments'. What he wants to hammer home is that rulers must never surrender to fortune, which is 'the arbiter of half the things we do, leaving the other half or so to be controlled by ourselves'.[43] Yet Machiavelli recognizes that fortune may succeed in overwhelming even the greatest leaders, few of whom have the capacity to transform their own characters to suit changing circumstances. He cites the example of Piero Soderini, *gonfaloniere* (Head of the Signoria) of Florence in the early 1500s, who governed his city with patience and humanity, allowing it to thrive. But in 1512, when brutal measures were required to defend the republic against its mortal enemies (foreign and domestic), he found it impossible 'to vary his procedure'.[44] Nevertheless, Machiavelli is careful 'not to rule out our free will' in the face of 'great changes and variations, beyond human imagining'.[45]

supernatural realm. The moral and religious beliefs that we regard as axiomatic are therefore our own, albeit unconscious, creation.

Machiavelli, according to Francesco De Sanctis, a nineteenth-century Hegelian liberal, gave expression to the emerging antagonism between theology and science, two 'ways of thinking and acting'. The scientific perspective was founded on the revolutionary idea that human consciousness is independent of any transcendent authority and is merely the self-knowledge of human beings acting in society and history to subdue nature for their own purposes. Machiavelli, in helping to pioneer this new outlook, thus represented 'the most profound negation of the Middle Ages'.[47] He sought truth on earth instead of in heaven.

4 • The Empirical Method

Because of his hostility to metaphysics, his refusal to appeal to something external to humankind and history, it is commonly assumed that Machiavelli's principal contribution to intellectual history was to base generalizations on the observation of events, not on deduction from first principles. It is said that he was a pioneer of the 'inductive method' – the idea of grounding knowledge on the collection, collation and analysis of what we call facts. This method is contrasted to the medieval habit of seeking explanations by a long process of inference and deduction. Like the ancient Greeks, medieval thinkers were interested in final causes, in what things were for, in purposes. Logic, not controlled observation, was the discipline for resolving theoretical disputes. While Machiavelli did not discard the idea that facts disclosed a deeper meaning, he used it – the argument runs – in a purely secular way, deducing general rules from singular historical situations. He thus emerges as the first political scientist. For Burnham, no stranger to hyperbole, he shared the methods of Galileo, Darwin and Einstein. His detailed conclusions might sometimes be wrong, but his methods were scientific. Political questions were to be settled by appeal to facts: if these disclose that successful rulers lie frequently and break treaties, then such a generalization takes precedence over an opposite law drawn from some metaphysical dogma which states that all men have an innate love of truth or that truth – in the long run – always triumphs over lies. When the facts decide, it is the principles that must be scrapped. Machiavelli, to Burnham, categorically rejected the type of theory that was simply the elaborate projection of wish fulfilment. Politics, in a manner identical to nature, operates according to fixed laws that impose limits on what we can or cannot achieve.[1]

By the middle of the last century, the elevation of Machiavelli to the same scientific status as Galileo had become a familiar theme among scholars of a positivist persuasion. According to Charles Singleton, Machiavelli was 'very much the experimental scientist, finding his laboratory either in the contemporary arena of political struggle or in history, ancient or recent . . . There, like a true scientist, he is interested in the particular instance only insofar as it may disclose a general principle.' Machiavelli's science, like Galileo's, required him to separate the object of study – in this case, human action – from religious imperatives and symbolism. Revealing no concern for man's soul or God's universal plan, Machiavelli confined his attention to '*bona exteriora*', to the external consequences of an agent's actions, thus ignoring '*bona interiora*', that is, what is good or not good for the agent in terms of his eternal destiny. Machiavelli, Singleton claims, was in this sense a 'revolutionary', who transformed 'traditional speculation on political order, on rule and rulers'.[2] Others agreed. In the opinion of Ernst Cassirer, the supposed prophet of evil was a pure scientist, 'the Galileo of politics', who 'studied political actions in the same way as a chemist studies chemical reactions . . . He never blames or praises political actions; he simply gives a descriptive analysis of them.'[3] Leonardo Olschki supported Cassirer's argument, claiming that Machiavelli, to a far greater extent than any of his contemporaries (including Leonardo da Vinci), possessed a refined scientific instinct. This is because, after the fashion of all great scientists, he started out with an axiomatic assumption that allowed his research findings to fit into a perceptible pattern. Galileo's controlling assumption was that 'matter is unalterable . . . eternal and necessary'. This axiom has its exact scientific counterpart in Machiavelli's fundamental premise that human nature is always and everywhere the same. If one assumes, as did the Florentine, that all men in all places pursue their own interests in a more or less rational way, then their actions become calculable and predictable. Galileo's concept of matter is no longer accepted in the way he intended, and Machiavelli's view of human nature is obviously open to question. Without these axiomatic propositions, however, neither man could have formulated his elaborate system of natural or political laws.[4]

The 'scientific' interpretation of Machiavelli, never universally shared, has become so unfashionable that it has virtually disappeared from the secondary literature. Nevertheless, in what follows, I shall mount a qualified defence of it against its critics, who fall into two basic categories. The first group argues that the idea of a 'political science' was the furthest thing from his mind. According to Maurizio Viroli, Machiavelli 'did not intend to found a science of politics, but to retrieve and refine the conception of political theory as an essentially rhetorical practice based upon historical knowledge and the ability to interpret actions, words and gestures'. He therefore 'did not collect or describe facts', and the Galilean method of inquiry based upon experiments, demonstrations and generalizations was 'totally alien from Machiavelli's style of thinking'. He wrote as an 'orator', or 'rhetorician', not as a scientist who wishes 'to investigate the eternal and immutable underneath the ever-changing flux of things'. To the contrary, he understood that political knowledge was always 'tentative and conjectural'. Deliberately immersing himself in a sea of particulars, he never searched for general laws of political behaviour. He sought only to produce coherent historical narratives, persuasive works of interpretative imagination.[5]

This interpretation relies on a very selective reading of the textual evidence. If Viroli were right, it would be hard to see why Machiavelli was forever concluding his arguments by announcing the discovery of 'a general rule, which never or rarely fails to apply' – or words to that effect.[6] *Pace* Viroli, he always seemed to be seeking the perennial in the transitory, the proven maxim that could help a statesman to curb a riot or gain an advantage over a rival. He was not primarily interested in the unique political event but in laws relating events. In his own words, he 'considers what has been' because he 'wishes to see what has to be'.[7] Moreover, his frequent references to 'natural necessity' when explaining human behaviour suggest that, for him, such behaviour was subject to rules and principles analogous to those which governed the natural world.[8] The very *form* of the *Discourses* belies Viroli's interpretation. Chapter headings usually consist of some political maxim or generalization: 'How Easily Men Can Be Corrupted', or 'One Often Obtains with Impetuosity and Audacity What One Would Never Have Obtained through Ordinary Modes'. In the chapter itself, Machiavelli treats each maxim or generalization as a hypothesis and seeks to verify it by citing historical examples. This was a new method of trying to discover truth, for earlier thinkers – while not necessarily averse to supporting a proposition by reference to historical models – had sooner or later appealed to an authority such as Scripture or Aristotle. Machiavelli's use of historical evidence may fail to convince, but his desire to derive general truths from historical facts is plain for all to see. Viroli views Machiavelli as a kind of verbal artist, seeking 'to persuade, to delight, to move, to impel to act'.[9] Since art appeals to our feelings, it is – Viroli seems to suppose – the very antithesis of science. But – as we have already seen in an earlier chapter – Italian Renaissance artists adopted a scientific view of the world, which not only complemented but enhanced the aesthetic quality of their work. They conceived of space and the physical world as phenomena which could be defined, measured and controlled by the human mind. Because truth to nature was their indispensable standard, this led to an emphasis on disciplined observation, on mathematical and experimental methods to achieve the correct proportions. Leonardo's paintings, for example, were informed by his studies of optics and anatomy. If Leonardo could be a scientist *and* an artist, why couldn't Machiavelli be a scientist *and* a rhetorician? Indeed, Galileo himself could be described as a rhetorician of sorts. As Maurice Finocchiaro shows, his *Dialogue on the Two Chief World Systems* does not simply reflect the activities of disciplined observation, logical reasoning and mathematical analysis; it also deploys rhetoric in its various senses of image projection, the creation of impressions, the use of persuasive analogies and eloquent expression. To a degree, this rhetorical dimension can be explained by the historical context. The book was written at a time when Galileo, as a Catholic, was bound by a decree issued by the Church in 1616 to the effect that one could neither hold nor defend the physical truth of Copernicanism. As his intention was to support Copernicus's geokinetic theory, he could not always say what he meant (or mean what he said). He found it necessary to disguise the substance of his position by conveying the message that he was merely *discussing* all the arguments for and against the two 'world-systems' (Ptolemaic and Copernican), without defending either one. While this pretence may account for the *Dialogue* being 'a goldmine of rhetoric', Finocchiaro makes the wider point that rhetoric is an essential component of scientific inquiry, especially when scientists disagree over fundamental issues or are faced with paradigm choice, that is, with having to choose between radically different world-views – Galileo's exact predicament. Contrary to Viroli's assumption, then, science and rhetoric are complementary rather than contradictory.[10]

The thesis that Machiavelli never aspired to be a scientist (in the conventional sense) is also defended by Benedetto Fontana, who is explicitly inspired by Gramsci's interpretation of Machiavelli as an 'active politician', fusing political analysis and political ideology. In Fontana's estimation, Machiavelli did not conceive knowledge as

a passive, merely reflecting product of reality that simply registers events . . . Machiavelli understands experience and 'empirical reality' not as an objective 'fact' that imposes itself on human beings . . . knowledge is informed by an active and critical orientation . . . His type of knowledge cannot be understood if it is separated from his 'intention'.

Knowledge, that is to say, is a product of the relation between human intentions – ends, goals, values – and 'the effective truth of things'. The '*dover essere*' (what ought to be) crucially shapes our knowledge of the '*essere*' (what is). According to Fontana, then, Machiavelli drew no hard-and-fast distinction between thought and reality, the inquiring mind and the object of inquiry. A value-neutral understanding of the world was therefore impossible, in his view.[11]

It is difficult to see how this interpretation can be squared with those passages where Machiavelli explicitly outlines his methodology. As Fontana sees it, the Florentine never intended to abandon the time-honoured unification of 'is' and 'ought', fact and value. But Machiavelli undoubtedly saw himself as an innovator, substituting 'things as they are' for 'things as . . . they are imagined'. He wanted to examine 'what is actually done', not 'what should be done'.[12] Such dichotomies – essential to modern scientific reasoning – directly contradict the Fontana/Gramsci interpretation. Machiavelli clearly distinguished the language of moral purpose from the language of empirical analysis. By positing a separation between normative and analytical political inquiry, he was, according to his own self-image, taking 'a path as yet untrodden by anyone'.[13] For him, the vast array of facts to be analysed included the whole of history from antiquity to the present. Understanding 'things as they are' obviously requires an understanding of 'things as they were'. History, he thought, could furnish a stable body of knowledge transcending the flux of events. But Machiavelli's historical method was not like that of Hegel – a mode of deriving from the order of historical evolution standards of valuation, scientific or ethical, by means of which the significance of particular stages in that evolution could be determined. The Hegelian method was interpretative – its purpose being to discover the foreordained 'meaning' of the 'historical totality'; Machiavelli's method was predictive and didactic. Studying the historical record would allow us to forecast with greater accuracy the consequences of different practices or courses of action – to negotiate the political world more effectively. Republican Rome, above all, provided later ages with a timeless model on which to base political actions and institutions. Whereas the Greek philosophers and Christian theologians sought truth in 'reason' or else 'faith', the new 'path' found its certainty in the examples of greatness or success supplied by history. Machiavelli noted a discrepancy between the present state of art, medicine and law, on the one hand, and the poverty of political knowledge, on the other. The former fields had succeeded in absorbing the experience of the past and adapting it to present circumstances. In politics, however, one finds 'neither prince nor republic' that turns to the ancients for instruction. To assume, as many do, that we can derive no practical lessons from the past is to argue that every situation in every age is essentially different, 'as if heaven, sun, elements, man had varied in motion, order, and power from what they were in antiquity'.[14] To Machiavelli, this refusal to learn from past experience or historical observation, this tendency to rely on 'intuition' and immutable Christian precepts, was nothing but a form of superstition – the very opposite of a scientific attitude. It was characteristic of the theological mentality he deplored, which declined to accept experience as objective fact and insisted on viewing the world through a prism of prior commitments.

Many commentators who accept that Machiavelli thought of himself as a detached, impartial scientific observer of events, past and present, nevertheless maintain that his self-image was based on delusion. Notwithstanding his intentions, they say, his new empirical 'path' rather resembled the old metaphysical path. While not altogether denying that he has a place in the great transition from teleological abstraction to empirical science, these commentators protest that he tended to wrest conclusions from recalcitrant evidence in a way that was hardly comparable to Galileo's methods of measurement and experimentation. Rather than sifting through the data and allowing generalizations to emerge, 'he is really only making deductions from classical theses concerning human nature or the historical process'.[15] On this interpretation, he looked to history for illustrations of general theorems that were already in his mind, not for data from which to draw such theorems. That Machiavelli 'transformed and stylized facts and events' in order to suit his purposes is now widely accepted.[16] Some unkind observers take an almost malicious pleasure in pointing out his non sequiturs and his selective way with evidence.[17]

Various explanations have been advanced for his alleged failure to discover genuine laws of political behaviour. One focuses on his excessive admiration for Roman values and institutions. He posited a simplistic contrast between ancient virtue and modern corruption, and too easily assumed that pagan modes and attitudes could be resurrected in the bourgeois, Christian Italy that so appalled him. These commitments or prejudices, it is argued, systematically distorted his vision. He was a dreamer, a man of intense passion, emotionally wedded to a revival of ancient glories.[18] This criticism is related to another one:

that Machiavelli had a defective sense of historical context, for – contrary to his assumptions – practices and behaviour that are appropriate in situation X are rarely appropriate in situation Y. Machiavelli disputed this because his historical reflections had convinced him that, essentially, human nature was always the same, always defined by the same passions and needs, and therefore likely to produce the same responses and outcomes in a variety of superficially different contexts:

> ... whoever wishes to see what has to be considers what has been; for all worldly things in every time have their own counterpart in ancient times. That arises because these are the work of men, who have and always had the same passions, and they must of necessity result in the same effect.[19]

What are these passions? Everywhere and at all times, men are driven by ambition, by love of power and by desire for possessions (*roba*), or greed.[20] Human psychology acts as a link or common denominator between past and present. Because of its constancy, historical incidents tend to fall into repeating patterns. Or, to put it another way, 'men are born, live, and die in accordance with an unvarying order'.[21] This, Garin points out, is Machiavelli's 'grand principle': *Eadem sunt omnia semper*.[22] If we dig deeply enough, supposedly unique situations will reveal themselves as typical occurrences. 'On this view of history', Butterfield observes, 'change is kaleidoscopic – there is reshuffling and recombination but no transformation of the constituent parts.'[23] The notion that all historical events are interchangeable was initially challenged by Machiavelli's friend, Francesco Guicciardini, a distinguished diplomat and historian in his own right. He did not share the Machiavellian penchant for describing things as 'natural' or 'necessary'; nor did he believe that present reality could be controlled in the light of ancient examples. Although he never questioned Machiavelli's view of the essential fixity of human nature, he nevertheless insisted that conditions and circumstances exhibit differences and exceptions that defeat all attempts to predict the precise consequences of any particular type of political practice or action:

> How wrong it is to cite the Romans at every turn. For any comparison to be valid, it would be necessary to have a city with conditions like theirs, and then to govern it according to their example. In the case of a city with different qualities, the comparison is as much out of order as it would be to expect a jackass to race like a horse.[24]

Where Machiavelli found general principles of absolute clarity, Guicciardini saw infinite complexities that refuted any simple rules.[25] On shifting sands like these, no science of statecraft could take hold. According to this still influential argument, Machiavelli's scientific ambitions foundered on the diversity and variety of human experience. His quixotic desire to interpret particular events as instances of general causal laws blinded him to the fact that government is not a science but an art – dependent on an imaginative grasp of contextual peculiarities. If his prejudices gained the upper hand, it was because he had set himself an impossible task to begin with. A rather different explanation for his scientific failings, recently developed at length by A. J. Parel, is that his mental outlook fell under the sway of the astrological nonsense that passed for serious thought during the Renaissance.[26] Astrology appeared then both as a 'science' of the stars and as an art of prognosticating their alleged effects on human affairs. Like so many of his contemporaries, Parel's Machiavelli believed that human behaviour was determined by celestial configurations associated with the images of pagan deities – Jupiter, Mercury, Venus, Mars and so on. He accepted the astrological conviction that 'the heavens' are the general cause of all the particular motions – human and natural – occurring in the sublunar world. That is to say, the motions of history as well as of states are subject to the motions of the heavens. Moreover, the celestial intelligences that guide the heavens love to tease or perhaps forewarn men about grave events through revelations, prodigies and other astral signs. Burnham proclaimed that there 'are no dreams or ghosts in Machiavelli', a thinker who 'lives and writes in the daylight world'.[27] But, in the opinion of Joseph Kraft, 'Machiavelli's daylight world was by no means ghostless'. It was a world of occult forces and interventions, of spirits and portents, far removed from the world of modern science.[28]

To the critics, then, Machiavelli did not take hold of political theory and transport it from speculative realms to a region of empirical observation. Instead, he was a pseudo-scientist who ultimately surrendered to dogma, who could 'see the shape of things only in the mould that his own mind had made for them'.[29] For these critics, his propensity to generalize was not so much scientific as artistic. Guided by preconceived ideas, he would see the general immanent in the particular and summarize his perception in brilliant epigrams and witty proverbs, reinforced by vivid portraits and images. If this is an accurate depiction of Machiavelli, then it would be wrong to describe him as a founder of the empirical method or as the originator of modern political science. But *is* it accurate? Or have the critics done him a disservice? First of all, those who belittle the scientific claims made on his behalf are often guilty of anachronism. Plamenatz, a notorious offender, complains that Machiavelli 'had no conception of scientific method, of the making and testing of hypotheses . . . no idea . . . that there are appropriate rules, that there is a proper method for testing [his] generalisations'.[30] But in Machiavelli's day, scientific method in our sense – deliberate, systematic, self-conscious – was only in its infancy. Copernicus's great works on astronomy, the turning point for modern science, were not published until after Machiavelli's death. In Machiavelli, as in Leonardo and (indeed) Copernicus, the nature of scientific method is not fully understood; some pre-scientific notions, held over from medieval and ancient metaphysics and theology, are retained. Copernicus himself still thought that the planets must move in circular orbits around the sun, because a perfect God would have created none but perfect motion in a circle for the heavenly bodies. Much is made of those few pages where Machiavelli revealed his belief in auguries; yet Johann Kepler, a great astronomer and one of the pioneers of modern science, a man born a century after Machiavelli, was among the best horoscope-casters of his time.[31] In any case, Parel exaggerates the significance of Machiavelli's leanings towards astrology. When the matter is explicitly considered in the *Discourses*, our author makes it clear that, for him, the existence of heavenly signs foretelling calamities or other momentous happenings is an *empirical fact* – and one that he professes himself unable to explain.[32] No doubt he confused popular fiction with established fact, but he shared this misapprehension with most of his educated contemporaries. In the same chapter, he mentions the common astrological belief that 'the air is full of intelligences' but pointedly refuses to commit himself to it.[33] Parel also reads too much into Machiavelli's apparent attribution of anthropomorphic qualities to 'the heavens' (*i cieli*). In Italy at the time, it was common to speak of these higher realms as if they had powers and intentions, and it is not clear whether Machiavelli's conformity to conventional speech patterns tells us anything about his cosmological system. Were his words meant to be taken literally? We have already seen how he exhibited the rhetorician's desire to address his audience in their own terms. Perhaps he was simply following a piece of advice he gave to the aspiring prince: that is, be 'a great liar', pretend to share the values and prejudices of your subjects even when you do not.[34] So far from being paralysed by superstition, Machiavelli wanted to manipulate it for the purposes of statecraft. Note his praise for Roman military chiefs who cynically interpreted unusual material events as favourable auguries in order to give psychological reassurance to discontented or hesitant troops.[35] But even if Machiavelli did, to some degree, fall under the spell of astrological speculation, this would not necessarily detract from his scientific reputation. It is perfectly possible for a scientist to adhere to superstitious beliefs, as long as these do not intrude upon his investigation of the physical universe. Newton's theology, for example, included a belief in witchcraft, but there are no pixies in the workings of the 'Newtonian world machine'.[36]

Another observation worth making, in defence of Machiavelli, is that his methodology was not nearly as unrefined as his critics would have us believe. It is true that his style of argumentation did not lend itself to subtlety. The 'on the one hand this and on the other hand that' approach, so dear to the hearts of academic social scientists, was not in keeping with his personality. He delighted in aphorisms and paradoxes, and was much given to axiomatic pronouncements. Emblematic of the way he thought was his disjunctive prose style, full of either/or formulations. This fondness for strong antitheses had the unfortunate effect of arbitrarily excluding every possibility lying between the poles of the either/or construction. Complex issues are thus reduced to artificial questions. Was virtue or fortune the cause of Rome's greatness? A finely shaded answer is effectively ruled out by the way the question is posed. This disjunctive technique is the appropriate formal expression of a mode of thought which assumes that a virtuoso politician will always make prompt and firm decisions, unencumbered by 'ifs', 'ands' and 'buts'. The 'middle way' is to be studiously avoided, irresolution spurned.[37]

Yet such crudity is not the whole story, for Machiavelli often displays a methodological sophistication and a respect for evidence that are curiously overlooked by his critics. One of their complaints, for example, is that he views antiquity as an infallible guide. But he quite explicitly acknowledges that those who laud ancient times frequently suffer from blind spots. Most history, we are reminded, is written by the victors or by those who depend on them, which means that the record of events available to us will, almost without exception, accentuate the positive and gloss over the negative.[38] Expressing self-doubt and self-awareness in equal measure, he writes: 'I do not know thus if I deserve to be numbered among those who deceive themselves; if in these discourses of mine I praise too much the times of the ancient Romans and blame ours.'[39] Although Machiavelli may not have entirely evaded the danger of which he speaks, his affinity for the Roman republic could hardly be described as 'slavish'.[40] In addition, let us not forget that the information available to him about the period was, of necessity, much scantier than our own – a point made in his defence by both Mosca and Pareto. As the latter remarked, 'one cannot blame Machiavelli for accepting the old Roman legends at face value. They were taken as history by everyone in his time.'[41] In assessing the Roman age, we have the accumulated benefits of patient documentary research by a veritable army of historians; he had no such advantage.

It is in any case wrong to assume that he derived his evidence exclusively or even mainly from antiquity. The Prince – to take an obviously important example – is full of references to recent history and contemporary politics. One distinguished scholar goes so far as to assert that this work 'reflects Machiavelli's fifteen years' experience in the chancery service', and that the various historical illustrations were strictly for rhetorical effect.[42] Whether or not this assessment is accurate, there is no denying that Machiavelli ordinarily supports his generalizations with examples drawn from several different periods of history. References to Roman and Greek history are often linked with references to Italian and European history comparatively close to his own time. It is reasonable to conclude – in defiance of his critics – that he wanted to guard against mistaking a type of behaviour characteristic of some particular period for a more general historical law. Machiavelli is also careful to point out that diverse conditions often require diverse forms of behaviour. He does not, as some of his critics suggest, put forward infallible maxims of universal applicability, as if contextual factors were of no account.[43] He explicitly acknowledges that it is often impossible to lay down inflexible rules because appropriate modes of action depend on circumstances; or else that it is impossible to formulate a definite precept without examining the details of the situation. Let us look at some examples. In The Prince, Machiavelli draws a contrast between a 'man who is made a prince by the favour of the people' and 'a man who has become a prince against the will of the people and by the favour of the nobles'. In both cases, the prince needs to secure the friendship of the people, though in the latter case it means winning them over. There are, says Machiavelli, 'many ways' in which a prince can do this, but these 'vary according to circumstances, so no definite rule can be given'.[44] Elsewhere, Machiavelli explores the more general question of how princes can maintain their power:

> To keep a secure hold on their states some princes have disarmed their subjects; some have kept the towns subject to them divided; some have purposely fostered animosity against themselves; some have endeavoured to win over those who were initially suspect; some have put up fortresses; some have razed them to the ground. It is impossible to give a final verdict on any of these policies, unless one examines the particular circumstances of the states in which such decisions have had to be taken.[45]

In the *Discourses*, he puts the question 'whether in a corrupt city one can maintain a free state' and concludes that 'it is almost impossible to give a rule for it, because it would be necessary to proceed according to the degrees of corruption'.[46]

Machiavelli's sensitivity to context is often implied rather than explicitly stated. Consider his analysis of 'the difficulties involved in holding a newly acquired state'. Centralized lands, like the kingdom of Turkey, are difficult to conquer (because the people are united in loyalty and subservience to the ruler) but easy to retain once occupied (because there are no alternative power centres which can provide a focal point for revolt). Contrariwise, feudal (or quasi-feudal) states, like France, are relatively easy to conquer (since malcontents among the barons can always be found to assist an outside force) but hard to subdue for any length of time (since nobles of ancient lineage, who are loved by their subjects and capable of mounting new insurrections, will remain). Those bent on conquest must bear these subtleties in mind and adjust their behaviour accordingly.[47] Even *within* states, the qualities necessary for successful leadership will vary with circumstances. Machiavelli praises Piero Soderini, leader of the ill-fated Florentine republic that was overthrown in 1512, for his 'humanity and patience', qualities which allowed his fatherland to prosper. But when times changed, and he needed to break with his humble ways, he did not know how to do it, 'so that he together with his fatherland was ruined'.[48]

What is more, when Machiavelli finds that two contrary lines of action have proved successful in analogous circumstances at different periods of the past, he uses this conflicting evidence as a cue for deeper analysis. In the *Discourses*, for example, he shows how Scipio made himself master of all Spain by his 'humanity and mercy', which won him the admiration and friendship of its peoples. Hannibal, on the other hand, attained the same dominance in Italy by very different means – 'cruelty, violence, robbery, and every type of faithlessness'. In attempting to explain the discrepancy, Machiavelli concludes that a conquering general has the option of making himself loved or feared. It is immaterial which of these two courses he takes, provided he is a man of sufficient abilities to correct whatever inconveniences may arise from the pursuit of either.[49]

Similarly, Machiavelli does not systematically ignore examples that might disprove his *regole generali*; his usual procedure is to explain why they are the exceptions that prove the rule. His reflections on mercenary soldiers nicely illustrate this point. Indulging in typical overstatement, he denounces such troops as 'useless and dangerous', since they are 'disunited, thirsty for power, undisciplined, and disloyal'. Yet the historical record forces him to concede that the Venetians and Florentines did extend their territories in the past through the use of mercenaries. While his explanations for this anomaly may not have been convincing (luck in the case of the Florentines; the modesty of their territorial ambitions in the case of the Venetians), the discussion demonstrates a willingness to confront and deal with contradictory evidence.[50]

None of this is to deny that he was sometimes economical with the truth. But even the most rigorous social scientist will occasionally jump through hoops to reconcile inconvenient data with his theoretical assumptions. 'Rescue hypotheses', to deal with apparent empirical counter-examples, are common even within the physical sciences. Moreover, it is necessary, once again, to look at Machiavelli in context. As an eminent specialist on the Renaissance observes:

> The mental outlook and habits of expression fostered by rhetorical training permeated the culture. Renaissance Italians were not burdened with the cult of sincerity so typical of modern democratic societies; for them, sincerity was a trope like any other. It was more important that speech be appropriate, elegant and effective than that it be strictly true. The rules of decorum in fact called for the *celatio* (concealment) or *suppressio* of the truth, even the *suggestio* of the false, in the appropriate rhetorical situation.[51]

However, while Machiavelli was a product of his culture, he also helped to create something new. For he insisted on contemplating human society and history as they were in reality, independently of metaphysical connections. He never argued about abstract truths. To him, the facts of political life were the only valid political arguments. For this reason, the key problems of traditional political philosophy – What is the best form of government? How would an ideal ruler behave? – held no interest for him. His *forma mentis*, being empirical, was downright hostile to such speculation, to 'things as they are imagined'. This is why he categorically rejected the rationalistic procedure – common to this day among political philosophers – of starting with first principles and logically deducing practical propositions from them. Yet this does not mean that he was opposed to abstraction as such. His assertions that all ages are of the same fundamental structure and that all men share an identical nature are empirical, inasmuch as they purport to describe an observable reality. But they also involve an element of abstraction from the variety and complications of actual experience. Abstraction in this sense does not necessarily destroy Machiavelli's scientific credentials. Analogous methods are followed in all sciences, both physical and social. When Newton introduced the idea of frictionless motion, bodies not acted upon by other forces, he did not imagine that such things existed exactly as he depicted them. It was a matter of abstracting for the sake of generalizing more adequately.[52]

But of all the criticisms of Machiavelli, perhaps the silliest is that he could not have been an objective empirical analyst of human affairs because of his political passion, his hatred of corruption and his desire to see the foreign invaders expelled from Italy. Let us concede that Machiavelli's intention was not merely to *describe* human behaviour, or to expound its enduring patterns or 'laws'. Insofar as he criticizes the contemporary world without mercy and perpetually tells the statesmen around him how they 'ought' to behave, he does not remain purely on the level of fact. His works, as everyone knows, abound in precepts, practical hints, counsels, prescriptions, warnings and useful maxims. The final chapter of *The Prince*, where realistic appraisal and detached advice give way to fervent nationalism, destroys any notion that Machiavelli was merely a cold-eyed technician, devoid of ideals and utterly cynical. But a passionate commitment to certain political ideas and principles is not incompatible with an equally passionate attachment to objective methods of analysis. His new 'path' required him to maintain a rigid distinction between 'fact' and 'value', to prevent his value-preferences from colouring his empirical analysis. No doubt he failed on occasion, but what strikes readers of Machiavelli is his remarkable degree of objectivity, his ability to set aside his personal bias in the pursuit of knowledge. Although, for example, he wanted the foreign invaders out of Italy, this did not prevent him from devising a set of rules, based on historical observation, that might enable such invaders to succeed in their nefarious ventures.[53] It was in the course of this discussion that he famously declared his neutrality towards Louis XII of France, whose aggrandizing adventures in Italy were so destructive: 'I do not mean to condemn the course of action taken by the king.'[54] Machiavelli could put himself into the shoes of any ruler, admirable or not, analyse the situation from his point of view, state the alternatives and prescribe the best moves.

It was probably unwise of Cassirer and others to compare Machiavelli to Galileo. The latter's methods of quantification and experimentation were not to the taste of the Florentine Secretary, who always retained the diplomat's fascination with the changing shapes and colours of political life, and consistently underlined the need for adaptability in the face of impermanence and uncertainty. Given the vicissitudes of fortune, and the infinitely variable quantities of *virtù*, it is unlikely that Machiavelli thought his 'laws' of political behaviour would yield exact predictions. The balance of probabilities, not eternal and immutable truth, was what he sought to discover. If it is accurate to describe him as a scientist, he was more like a physician than a physicist, diagnosing his patient's illness and then prescribing a remedy based on what has worked in the past. Indeed, he thought of his endeavours in precisely these terms, comparing the body politic to the human body and likening himself to a doctor called upon to cure political disorders.[55] Medicine, of course, is an inexact science. Symptoms can be interpreted in different ways, and remedial measures can be ineffective if the doctor has made an incorrect diagnosis or if the patient's physiological functions are in any way peculiar. The comparison can be pressed further. Some people make the unthinking assumption that scientific inquiry cannot be motivated by practical goals – or at least they make this assumption with respect to political thinkers who aspire to be scientific. Machiavelli is not the only target here. How often are we told that Marx or Pareto could not have been scientific because they had political axes to grind. But this is tantamount to saying that medical researchers are not scientists. Are those seeking to develop drugs for Aids or cancer less than scientific simply because they are driven by the practical aim of extending human life? Science is not a passive activity; it involves constraining nature to give answers to questions of our own determining. Only when the analyst allows his goals to distort the facts do such value commitments become an impediment to scientific objectivity.

All things considered, it would not appear excessive to concur with Baron's judgement that Machiavelli 'laid the groundwork for the transformation of cosmology'. He represented the transition from a static/theological to a dynamic/scientific vision of life, where truth is dependent on the observation of reality and nothing else.[56] He searched not for 'final' causes, emanating from God's design for the universe, but for 'efficient' causes, grounded in human dispositions and actions. Explanation, for him, consisted in showing an event to be an instance of a law-like regularity between facts. The question 'why' was replaced by the question 'how'.

Even if we praise Machiavelli for his empirical method, his objectivity and his aspiration to gain predictive knowledge of political phenomena, we might still recoil from the very idea of a science of politics. Was Machiavelli engaged in a fruitless quest? Physicists or astronomers can assume that the same causes will always have the same effects. They may predict with absolute certainty a future event: for instance, an eclipse of the sun or the moon. Human behaviour is much less predictable. Even the most ardent champions of the unity of scientific method will concede that social science has to deal with laws of greater complexity than those of the natural world; or, rather, with a co-mingling of the effects of various laws, making it hard to disentangle one set of effects from another. Neither – for obvious reasons – is it able to isolate effects by controlled experiment. Consider the case of Pareto, noted for his positivist approach to the study of politics and society. Notwithstanding his determination to model his analysis on the methods and assumptions of the physical sciences, he was forced to acknowledge that social scientific inquiry is 'contingent, relative, yielding results that are just more or less probable'.[57] Others would go further and question whether the study of politics can be scientific at all. As we have seen, Machiavelli himself, when confronted by complex and multiple permutations of circumstances, was often reluctant to formulate general 'laws'. Indeed, his political *experience* was in flagrant contradiction with his general scientific principles. Experience had taught him that even the most artful and cunning schemes are liable to failure; they may suddenly and unexpectedly be thwarted by *Fortuna*, whose capricious ways can mock all our calculations. Equally at odds with his search for general empirical truths was the powerful role he assigned to *virtù*, to personality, in shaping human affairs. Are 'great men' subject to the 'laws' of politics, or are they not? Machiavelli never resolved this ambiguity, possibly because there is no resolution. In the sphere of politics, the principle of universal determinism is certainly problematic, and for reasons that Machiavelli himself supplies. This does not mean that a science of politics is impossible, but it must recognize its limitations and somehow 'build in' humanity's magical powers of self-transformation.

A final doubt must be registered about the key assumption that underlies Machiavelli's methodology: that human nature is uniform in time and space, thus ensuring that all societies are essentially identical. The ancient Greeks and Romans were, in his eyes, much the same as the Italians of his own day. Lacking any discernible conception of moral and cultural change, he could identify history with nature: historical events, like processes in the natural world, repeat themselves endlessly; the same situations occur again and again; whatever happens is therefore typical and usually falls under a general rule. The idea of history as something essentially unchanging was taken for granted by Renaissance humanists. While they paid some attention to historical context when interpreting texts, they exhibited no real feeling for historical development. In this respect, too, Machiavelli was a child of his time. In applying his methodology, he did, as we have seen, show sensitivity to variations in circumstances, but the absence of any sense that society changes from age to age, that it is difficult to extrapolate general truths or rules of conduct from the past, especially the distant past, will always cast a dark shadow over the validity of his conclusions. Adopting a scientific approach is one thing; arriving at the right answers quite another.

But what people find particularly disturbing about Machiavelli's 'scientific' findings is the way they transmute into a normative theory. Philosophers may insist on a rigid distinction between fact and value, but in practice our scheme of values will always be heavily influenced by our understanding of how the world actually works. Marx was explicit about this: the only possible justification for an ideal is its historical necessity. Communism is 'good' only because scientific analysis tells us that it is the natural outcome of capitalism's inherent and insoluble contradictions. Similarly, because Machiavelli's empirical observations confirmed that the political world was a nasty place, it became imperative for rulers to behave in a nasty way. Machiavelli's point of departure was a strict separation between 'what is' and 'what ought to be', but he ended up deriving the latter from the former. This apparent anomaly would not have troubled him; for he thought that values and ideals, while they are distinct from facts, should nevertheless be based on facts, and not on utopian dreams or wishful thinking. Our normative preferences should not intrude upon our scientific analysis of the facts, but these preferences would be worthless if they were not compatible with the facts.

5 • Political Realism

Machiavelli's realism, as much as his commitment to the empirical method, stemmed from his rejection of metaphysics and teleology. If the universe is not governed by Reason or Mind, if the structure of reality is basically a system of physical motion, then effective truth, practical reality, is all there is. There is no natural order of the soul, and therefore no natural hierarchy of values. In determining how people *ought* to live, we must be guided by how they *do* live, by their actual thoughts and behaviour. With scientific detachment, the objective observer sweeps away the web of illusion people spin round themselves and concentrates on factual evidence. What, then, are we talking about when we talk about politics? Humanity's search for the ideally good society? Not according to Machiavelli, for whom politics was primarily the struggle for power. In the turmoil of Renaissance Italy, no rulers or diplomats seriously doubted that force rather than God's will was the key to understanding politics. But few people, before Machiavelli, were openly willing to define the state as a 'power system'. Instead, it was conventionally and officially seen as an embodiment of universal purposes, as a system of 'justice' or 'authority', ordained by God. Accordingly, political thinkers showed less interest in how man actually behaves than in his 'end' or destiny, together with its implications for the rights and duties of rulers and subjects. Machiavelli was tired of political literature that valued abstract speculation over practical experience – that envisaged imaginary princes living in imaginary states. He expressed this view with memorable bluntness in *The Prince*:

. . . in discussing this subject, I draw up an original set of rules. But since my intention is to say something that will prove of practical use to the inquirer, I have thought it proper to represent things as they are in real truth, rather than as they are imagined. Many have dreamed up republics and principalities which have never in truth been known to exist; the gulf between how one should live and how one does live is so wide that a man who neglects what is actually done for what should be done learns the way to self-destruction rather than self-preservation.[1]

This quotation incorporates three distinct propositions, each of which will be discussed in turn: (1) human beings are not what they seem; despite their professions of Christian goodness, they are generally wicked and unreliable; (2) ideal projections – depictions of perfect states, perfect rulers, perfect citizens – are both absurd and harmful; and (3) security – the precondition of all other political goods – often requires actions at variance with traditional biblical morality.

Proposition 1

Machiavelli's view of human nature was relentlessly pessimistic: 'One can make this generalisation about men: they are ungrateful, fickle, liars, and deceivers, they shun danger and are greedy for profit'.[2] Elsewhere, he declares, more succinctly, that 'all men are bad'.[3] Human beings will never be as they are described by those who idealize them. Indeed, Machiavelli's view of human nature was Hobbesian – before Hobbes. Nature, we learn, 'has created men so that they are able to desire everything and are unable to attain everything'. As the desire is always greater than the power of acquiring, 'the result is discontent with what one possesses'. But since all men want more than they have, they are simultaneously frightened that the depredations of others will deprive them of whatever goods they do possess, however meagre or unsatisfying. The explosive combination of insatiable ambition and endemic suspicion is the root cause of political enmities and conflict, within and between states.[4] This way of looking at reality appears to undermine classical and Christian morality, which conceived of natural desires as limited and capable of satisfaction through the principle of reciprocity. Since there is no objective source of conflict in the world, concord is rooted in the true nature of things. But Machiavelli, holding as he does that desire is inherently insatiable, is saying that the human condition is one of discontent and competition rather than natural harmony. Conflict is not the result of subjective error or moral weakness; it is not corrigible through discipline or reason or education. Human order therefore becomes problematic. The security and integrity of the collectivity are perpetually endangered by both internal foes, determined to destroy existing arrangements, and external foes, bent on expansion at its expense. At the international level, war and violence are ever-present realities, for if a state 'will not molest others, it will be molested'.[5] Machiavelli rejected the conventional idea of an orderly world, where every person or community fits into a larger whole as a piece in a jigsaw. To the contrary, the world is fluid, dangerous – and self-assertion is necessary if one is not to be swallowed up by predators. The meek will never inherit the earth. Political life is, at bottom, a gladiatorial arena where the strong subdue the weak and obtain preferential access to the limited number of goods.[6]

Humans are reluctant, though, to accept this harsh truth, and try to soften it by creating an illusory world of ideals that give a spurious moral justification to our predatory instincts. Even if society's rulers do not themselves believe in these doctrines, they would be well-advised to pretend otherwise; for it is a Machiavellian theme that a state founded on common values and cultural traditions has a greater chance of survival than one founded almost exclusively on naked force.[7] It is rarely sufficient, in Machiavelli's opinion, for political leaders to behave like lions; they must also possess the cunning of a fox, an ability to manipulate prevailing images and emotive symbols. Fraud, as well as force, is a necessary component of effective government.[8] Machiavelli showed great foresight in recognizing that 'the people' were an increasingly powerful factor in modern society, a constituency that had to be satisfied, even in principalities or kingdoms.[9] But – rather like modern politicians – he had limited faith in the rational or self-governing capacities of ordinary folk, for they 'are so simple, and so much creatures of circumstance, that the deceiver will always find someone ready to be deceived'. Humans in general will judge a ruler or politician by his 'image': 'Everyone sees what you appear to be; few experience what you really are.' The 'common people' are easily bamboozled because they are too preoccupied with their own concerns to analyse the words and deeds of a man they have been taught to trust. In the absence of an obvious cause for suspicion, they take professed motives and intentions at their face value. The inevitable disparity between the ideals of the civilization and the practices necessary to survive is a principal source of both self-deception and deception of others. While the mass of people can make or break regimes, they are like malleable matter, ready to respond to the shaping hand of the ruler/artist. And since they are 'always impressed by appearances', it is necessary for a successful leader to be 'a great liar and deceiver' (*gran simulatore e dissimulatore*). In this sense, appearances constitute the reality of politics – a form of activity predicated on concealment and the projection of images.[10]

Political analysts, however, are obliged to penetrate the fog of pious words and grand principles that enables politicians to befuddle the masses. Following his own advice, Machiavelli took mischievous pride in demystifying the deeds of the ancient Romans, who were, to his mind, great exemplars of dissimulation, the first 'foxes', confounding their external enemies with the most devious diplomacy imaginable.[11] The 'foxes' of antiquity would not have thanked their admirer for this description of their exploits. That deceitfulness could be an aspect of political virtue was simply unthinkable to the Romans. Neither in Virgil's epic poetry nor in Livy's epic history was the dissembler or fraudster allowed to figure other than as a villain. Stoic philosophy, moreover, always sided with the 'good' over the merely useful. Even in their most jingoistic moments, ancient writers were anxious to depict Roman expansion as the divinely ordained extension of law and civilization across the known world. But, for Machiavelli, we will never understand the Romans if we look at them through spectacles coloured by their myths and illusions. Cold-eyed analysis indicates, for example, that 'they made almost all their wars taking the offensive against others and not defending against them'.[12] Where Cicero saw ancient people freely welcoming the Romans because they were the embodiment of justice and fair play, Machiavelli saw the Romans devouring their neighbours through self-conscious power politics. The force and fraud Cicero hated were, in his estimation, the heart and soul of Roman greatness. But while Machiavelli advocated a judicious combination of the two essential methods of rule, he left us in no doubt which took priority. All the deceit or fraud in the world will not obviate the need for force, because men will 'use the malignity of their spirit whenever they have a free opportunity for it'.[13] To him, fear – dread of punishment – rather than love or solidarity is the ultimate foundation of political order. The sword is sharper than the word.[14]

Although Machiavelli believed that contemporary Italy could be regenerated through a 'rebirth' of the political wisdom and military ethos of ancient Rome, he never advocated a simple imitation of antiquity. His classicism was realistic. He recognized that the Romans themselves were flexible enough to adapt to circumstances and did not permit rigid principles to cramp their style. Nor did he think that ancient Rome offered a perfect model that could endure without change and adaptation. Thus we come to his disdain for utopian ideals.

Proposition 2

Inherent in Machiavelli's view of the human condition is that states will always be struggling against the tendencies of dissolution. The natural selfishness of men will regularly subvert the state, reduce it to chaos, and transform it into something different. The perpetual flux of human affairs rules out the possibility of a perfect state as timeless as a geometric theorem.[15] However, when Machiavelli says that 'human things are always in motion', there is no suggestion of evolutionary progress.[16] For him, human history is a ceaseless process of deterioration and renewal, a never-ending cycle of recurrent sequences:

> For Nature having fixed no sublunary Things, as soon as they arrive at their acme and perfection, being capable of no farther ascent, of necessity they decline. So, on the other side, when they are reduced to the lowest pitch of disorder, having no further to descend, they recoil again to their former perfection . . . Virtue begets Peace; Peace begets Idleness; Idleness, Mutiny; and Mutiny, Destruction: and then *vice versa*, that Ruin begets Laws; those Laws, Virtue; and Virtue begets Honour and good Success.[17]

Because human nature alone remains fixed and invariable throughout the centuries, the pattern of social and political change occurs again and again in history, so that by studying the past we learn also about the present and the future. The pattern is familiar to any historian: civilizations arise, prosper, become corrupt and disintegrate. Machiavelli, exhibiting a precocious form of Hegelian dialectical reasoning, claimed that the very virtues of the good state contain the seeds of its own destruction. For the strong and flourishing state is feared by its neighbours and consequently left in peace. But, alas, 'Peace begets Idleness; Idleness, Mutiny; and Mutiny, Destruction'. Or, as he puts it elsewhere, 'the cause of the disunion of republics is usually idleness and peace; the cause of union is fear and war'.[18] Freed from the tensions and rigours of war, the populace acquires a taste for luxury and licence. Selfish instincts are given free rein. In the absence of external enemies, internal conflicts develop from the most trivial causes and are magnified out of all proportion. Unity and discipline break down; corruption and effeminacy become rife. Decline is inevitable. However, 'Ruin begets Laws; those Laws, Virtue; and Virtue begets Honour and good Success'. Either through conquest or internal regeneration, a new, leaner and hungrier state or civilization will eventually replace the degenerate one, only to follow the same road to ruin.

The cycle of growth, decay and renewal is of course the basic law of nature. Typically, Machiavelli argues by analogy from the biological to the political. This does not mean, however, that he denies free will, or the role of conscious intervention in the historical process. The cycle of change is explained by traits that distinguish man from the natural world. While human greed and self-obsession bring about political decline, human ingenuity and will-power will usually generate a revival – unless a dissolute state is first devoured by a neighbouring state, which may be experiencing its 'acme and perfection'. The ascent from 'Ruin' to 'Honour and good Success' requires the intervention of a wise and dictatorial ruler, who may have to resort to brutal actions to restore political health: 'This should be taken as a general rule: that it never or rarely happens that any republic or kingdom is ordered well from the beginning or reformed altogether anew outside its old orders unless it is ordered by one individual.'[19] A people who have fallen prey to self-indulgent passions cannot spontaneously transform themselves into a body of virtuous citizens. This is a task for special men, men of *virtù* in the distinctively Machiavellian sense. Even in a well-run republic, according to Machiavelli, the vast majority of citizens will be dull-witted, passive and self-absorbed. Even in these republics, it is the talented and purposeful few who prevent society from collapsing into chaos and squalor. In his opinion, society will always be divided into those who command and those who serve, regardless of the constitutional order. 'For in all republics, ordered in whatever mode', we are told, 'never do even forty or fifty citizens reach the ranks of command.'[20] Machiavelli bore no hostility to popular participation when it was mediated by representatives of superior intellect and virtue. Yet he never doubted 'the uselessness of a multitude without a head'.[21] Equality in any real sense was neither possible nor desirable. A people can be 'great' only insofar as they become faithful (if pale) copies of their 'betters'. *Real* power, even in the most 'democratic' of republics, is always in the hands of the few. Machiavelli's imagery effectively conveys his political vision. Throughout his works, the Aristotelian pairing of 'matter' with 'form' incessantly recurs; and wherever the theme is present, the message is the same: that the people, an undifferentiated mass of matter, are nothing without the form stamped upon them by the elite.[22] He underlines the point with images of the builder, the sculptor and the architect working with their materials.[23]

In light of his insistence on a clear distinction between rulers and ruled, it is hard to see why some commentators persist in portraying

Machiavelli as a champion of democracy in its purest sense. On their reading, he is more of an idealist than a realist. Viroli maintains, for example, that his hero wants 'a community of free and equal individuals', whose distinctive feature is the 'inter-changeability of rulers and ruled'.[24] Fontana goes even further, claiming that 'the Machiavellian form of ruling' is 'based on the ability to "reason without the use of authority and force"' and dedicated to overcoming 'relations of domination'. In Machiavelli's 'new and radical notion of what it means to rule', 'force and authority are excluded' and replaced by 'a relation of mutual recognition and equal speech or discourse'.[25] Where is the evidence for such an interpretation? While there is no doubt that Machiavelli advocated equality before the law and equal access to political office, he never believed that *de jure* equality could become *de facto* equality, or that the people, gullible as they were, could be magically transformed into what Fontana refers to as 'a self-determining subject', committed to 'self-reflection' and 'rational discourse'.[26] Perhaps Machiavelli could be considered a democrat if we were less stringent about what that appellation entails. After all, democracy as we know it is perfectly compatible with strong leadership and mass apathy. But let us not forget that he advocated civic equality for all *citizens*, and not for all adults living within the state. The Florentine republic he served had 90,000 inhabitants, and some 3,200 citizens. Within that citizen body were included most native Florentines carrying on an independent business, and the excluded, apart from women and children, were mostly foreign residents, servants and labourers. Machiavelli never proposed reforms to extend the rights of citizenship to a larger percentage of the population. It is also worth pointing out that the ancient Romans he so admired were never remotely democratic in the modern sense, and would have wholeheartedly rejected the political egalitarianism that Viroli and Fontana attribute to Machiavelli. As F. E. Adcock, a student of Roman political thought, reminds us: 'The Romans did not ever believe in what has been called parity of esteem, and they no more believed that all men were equally suited to govern the state than that all men were equally tall.' While their republican procedures included a formal 'democratic element', this remained 'latent', and the 'day-to-day reality in the Roman State was the authority of the nobility vested in its vehicle the Senate'.[27] Even the democratic element, the tribunate, represented only citizens, who were a small proportion of the population.

Although Machiavelli was no egalitarian, he was partial to republics and republicanism. But this preference owed nothing to abstract idealism, to visions of human excellence or of a community united in pursuit of the 'good life'. Values, he thought, must be aligned with facts. Hopes for the future must always be tempered by the limitations of human nature and the fragility of all human constructions. Politics, for Machiavelli, is a matter of managing or reducing inconvenience and pain, not eliminating it. Political choice characteristically involves identifying the lesser of two evils.[28] The best state is best because historically tried and proven, not best in an abstract and illusionary sense. If he prefers republics to monarchies, it is purely for practical reasons. Where circumstances are appropriate, the former can produce the optimal combination of security and prosperity – the main goals, to him, of any political system. Why is this so?

A good monarch is rare, two good monarchs in succession defy all the odds, but a 'virtuous succession' of able rulers will always exist in a well-ordered republic, since the field of recruitment is wide.[29] Moreover, Machiavelli observes, princes fear men of talent and boldness, and do not, as a rule, offer them preferment. The corrupt and the incompetent thus acquire disproportionate influence, insidiously undermining standards throughout society. In a free city, however, where no single person enjoys absolute authority, men of stature compete openly and on strictly relevant grounds. Through this process of competition, they 'police' one another, thereby preserving the highest possible standards of probity and efficiency.[30] Also, while the common people may not be very bright or well-informed, they are generally less capricious than princes. Machiavelli thus contests the conventional view that 'nothing is more vain and inconstant than the multitude'. To the contrary, history teaches us that princes show less respect for constitutional or economic order than do 'peoples', who, wishing only to live in security, usually adopt a 'prudent' attitude to public affairs. This is what Machiavelli has in mind when he, rather uncharacteristically, likens the 'voice of a people' to 'that of God'.[31] He may have been guilty of rhetorical excess here; given that, a few chapters earlier in the *Discourses*, he had spoken of how 'grave men of authority' can and must check the 'fury' of 'an excited multitude' – the implication being that such multitudes are not uncommon.[32] In the later chapter, however, Machiavelli points out that princes, too, are liable to errors caused by passion, and that these are more frequent than those of the multitude. This is not all. Popular institutions tend to promote patriotism and habits of civility, and thereby diminish the need for extreme acts of repression. The feeling of security created by the rule of law allows individuals to pursue their personal projects in an adventurous and innovative spirit. Republics can also adapt better to changing times, since hidebound or idiotic rulers face the prospect of dismissal at regular intervals. Finally, in monarchical systems, the common good is often confused with the private good of the prince, whereas the whole purpose of a republic is to maximize the good of the majority, 'against the disposition of the few crushed by it'.[33] Essential to the common good, according to Machiavelli, is territorial expansion, and republics have the virtue of being inherently predatory: 'it is seen through experience that cities have never expanded either in dominion or in riches if they have not been in freedom.'[34]

The 'common good' is a term that appears frequently in the *Discourses*. However, whereas Aristotle had assumed that the common good was qualitatively different in nature from that of the individual, Machiavelli took the notion to mean a preponderance of interests and forces within the community. In other words, he abandoned the classical and medieval idea of the community as a natural unity. Society, as he conceived it, was naturally divided into competing interests and could never be kept to a perfect unity of purpose. The Aristotelian goal of civic concord, *homonoia*, the union of souls in a way of life, was quite foreign to Machiavelli. If the classical and medieval attitude towards conflict can be symbolized by Cicero's principle of *concordia ordinum*, Machiavelli's position is represented by *concordia discors* (or 'asocial sociability').[35] Unity is artificial and constantly under threat; it comes from a resolution of conflicting interests. Politics, on this conception, is a kind of dialectical process characterized by a clash of opposites, their temporary reconciliation in an uneasy social balance, and then the need to readjust the equilibrium because of new causes of conflict.

While the architects of utopianism place man outside history in a social world free of conflicts and tensions so that he can live in perfect harmony, Machiavelli accepts the inevitability of man living in time and being subject to its ravages. Continuous strife is an abiding condition of political life. This is a brute fact, but we should welcome it and recognize its creative possibilities. Most intriguing, in this respect, is Machiavelli's discussion of 'the tumults between the nobles and the plebs' in Roman times. With scant regard for conventional wisdom, he identifies the glory of Rome with the perennial conflict between her social classes. People who condemn such discord – all of Machiavelli's contemporaries – 'do not consider that in every republic are two diverse humors, that of the people and that of the great, and that all laws that are made in favour of freedom arise from their disunion'.[36] This is what we would now describe as a classic pluralist argument. Sociologically, the foundation of liberty is a balance of competitive social forces. As human beings are naturally selfish and anxious, dissension is inevitable. But the continuing clash of opposing groups, if moderated by a common devotion to the *patria*, generates an equally common devotion to liberty. For, where bargaining and compromise are necessary, there develops a climate of tolerance, of give and take, of live and let live. Calls for unity are, to Machiavelli, a cover for the suppression of dissent, for the triumph of one social interest, one absolute principle. Roman class divisions, he adds, were also conducive to social morale and civic responsibility. Each class gained from the other: the people were elevated to grandeur and heroism when they imitated the nobles, while the nobles, constantly menaced by the people, felt obliged to channel their energies into planning the conquest of other city-states rather than plotting to destroy one another.[37] Machiavelli is clear, though, that beneficial conflict can exist only in a *healthy* republic, where most citizens retain a sense of civic spirit and duty, and where in times of danger they are willing to sacrifice narrow self-interest for the public utility. This is why he thought that conflict in Florence had generally taken the malignant form of factionalism and anarchy. In expatiating on the history of his native city, Machiavelli implies that conflict between *classes* (*umori*) is natural and potentially the guarantor of a thriving social and political existence, whereas the conflicts that Florence specialized in – between families, clans, patronage systems – are 'dangerous and fatal'.[38] Classes squabble about different variations of the common good; 'factions' seek to further their own petty and private interests. Nevertheless, conflict between the 'two diverse humors' can also be destructive unless checked and channelled by legal mechanisms. Machiavelli thinks it self-evident that, if the constitution is so arranged that one or other of these *umori* is allowed total control, the republic will sink into corruption. If an aristocratic form of government is set up, the rich will rule in their own interests; if there is democracy the poor will despoil the rich and reduce the polity to penury and licentiousness. The solution, Machiavelli argues, is the Roman one of a mixed constitution, aiming for a balanced equilibrium between opposing social forces. Human selfishness cannot be extirpated, but it can be tamed and put to productive use by a good legal order.[39]

Reading *The Prince* in isolation might lead one to conclude that Machiavelli preferred absolute monarchy to republican forms of governance. He did not. His conclusion that none but a prince, unfettered by scruple or opposition, could save Italy was dictated by evidence rather than principle. In Machiavelli's view, political choices, like normative theorizing itself, must reflect 'things as they are in real truth, rather than as they are imagined'.[40] Although there was nothing utopian about a republic, it was not possible in all circumstances. Indeed, in times of 'urgent dangers', even established republics should emulate the Romans by appointing a temporary dictator with the right 'to do everything without consultation, and to punish everyone without appeal'.[41] For Machiavelli, the theoretical question of 'who should rule' could not be divorced from the practical question of whether whoever is ruling is doing so effectively. The unity of theory and practice was his intent. Theory must descend from the ethereal heights of philosophy into the mundane world of affairs. It was this intention that drove him to challenge an assumption fundamental to western political thought and scarcely questioned by any of his scholastic or humanist predecessors: that political success and the happiness of the people could be guaranteed by the exercise of traditional moral virtues. This brings us to the final proposition.

Proposition 3

Machiavelli is commonly assumed to be the inventor of *ragion di stato*, but this is not quite true. Political realism was already in the air, as we have seen, and the word 'necessity' dominated the administration and diplomacy of Italian city-states during the fifteenth century. Thinkers and historians, too, apart from Machiavelli, asserted that the only way to learn about politics was through experience. The name Guicciardini springs to mind here – a man who assumed the priority of ad hoc solutions over general principles. Even medieval legal theorists and canonists endorsed the idea that 'necessity has no law' to justify the extraordinary acts to which a ruler might resort through force of circumstances. St Thomas Aquinas, for example, recognized that very often the good that is sought in politics is not 'good simply' (*bonum simpliciter*) but 'good with reservations' (*bonum secundum quid*).[42] Neither was Machiavelli the first person to discover that immoral behaviour often pays dividends. Chabod makes an interesting distinction between 'virtual' and 'theoretical' Machiavellianism.[43] The former – disregarding moral rules, acting out of expediency, or with a devilish or manipulative cunning – has been practised by monarchs and other rulers from time immemorial. When such behaviour was confined to 'exceptional' circumstances and dedicated to the pursuit of religiously laudable goals, even the most rigorous of churchmen was willing to condone it as properly Christian. But Machiavelli transformed 'virtual' Machiavellianism into a theoretical precept of universal validity. Actions once deemed exceptional or deviant were now declared commonplace and even admirable. What horrified Machiavelli's readers was not so much his *description* of political life – with its crimes and treacheries – as his apparent determination to teach the *art* of political criminality and treachery, as if the usual moral guidelines had no relevance to politics. He was not talking about the occasional bending of rules, nor about extreme situations requiring extreme measures. Political choice, as Machiavelli presents it, *always* seems to be between evils. Political affairs are perpetually desperate because of the venality and depravity of mankind. Securing a good end – an island of political security in a sea of corruption – will *normally* necessitate violence and betrayal in some shape or form. Political leaders who fight shy of this 'truth', who flaunt their 'clean hands', will condemn their citizens or subjects to untold misery.

The outrage caused by Machiavelli's writings, once they were published and digested, is easy to understand; for they posed a mortal challenge to a set of assumptions that were fundamental to both classical and Christian political thought, and taken as gospel by earlier humanists. From the time of Plato, philosophers had argued that there was an unbreakable connection between nature, happiness and virtue. Nature was benign, it wanted people to be happy, and provided rules of moral conduct – discoverable by Reason or revelation – to achieve this aim. An analogous system governed political life. States were natural institutions. If they were to be happy, then rulers had to act according to the moral laws that underpinned private life. They had to act virtuously (in the pre-Machiavellian sense). True, this set of assumptions described an ideal situation rather than actual reality. As we have seen, it was accepted that, in practice, individual morality and public morality might need to diverge on occasion. But Machiavelli went beyond this concession; he was apparently saying that, in politics at least, there was little or no connection between what is moral and what is useful. Even his friend Guicciardini, who was happy to use the political vocabulary of power and domination, found Machiavelli disturbing, accusing him of being 'extremely partial to extraordinary and violent methods'.[44] Indeed he was. Consider his advice on how to unite a divided city where factionalism has given rise to violence. The only logical mode of proceeding, we learn, is 'to kill the heads of the tumults'; but because 'such executions have in them something of the great and the generous', a 'weak republic', whose leaders have been enfeebled by a Catholic education, will deem them 'inhuman' and 'impossible'. The example he gives is the indulgence shown by the Florentine rulers of Pistoia to the warring parties in that town.[45] Where other observers saw wisdom and Christian forbearance, Machiavelli saw contemptible weakness. He divorced the *virtù* appropriate to princes and rulers from the conventional catalogue of Christian and classical virtues, and sought to constrain their behaviour solely by reasons of state. There is a brief but famous passage in the *Discourses* that succinctly conveys his indifference towards the ethical lexicon that was common in early modern Europe:

> the fatherland is well defended in whatever mode one defends it, whether with ignominy or with glory . . . where one deliberates . . . on the safety of the fatherland, there ought not to enter any consideration of either just or unjust, merciful or cruel, praiseworthy or ignominious.[46]

Prior to Machiavelli, 'realism', as conventionally understood, was a matter of adapting natural law or God's law to the realities of political life. On Machiavelli's definition, realism meant that Christian morality, with its dichotomies of good and evil, right and wrong, had no place in political life.

Machiavelli's many detractors have portrayed him as an advocate of political immorality. A more generous interpretation – the one advanced by Croce – sees him as a defender of political *a*morality. Politics, that is to say, answers to its own logic, follows its own rules, and judges actions in accordance with its own standards of success or failure. It is – to borrow a phrase from Nietzsche – beyond good and evil. Croce maintains that Machiavelli was torn and tormented by the necessity of doing evil for the sake of good. He did not, on this account, deny the validity of Christian morality but reluctantly accepted that men with public responsibilities must dirty their hands in a way that could never be justified in the sphere of private relationships.[47]

Croce's thesis became something of a cliché in the secondary literature

until the late 1960s, when it was forcefully disputed by Isaiah Berlin.[48]
He pointed out that, however troubled Croce may have been by the
demonic demands of power, Machiavelli's thought displayed no such
anguish. Machiavelli did not have to suspend morality in order to be
Machiavelli; he simply had to affirm the tenets of *pagan* morality.
Whatever favours the interests of the community is, to a pagan, morally
good. Therefore a pagan statesman can perform Machiavellian deeds
with a clear conscience, for he knows morality is on his side. Machiavelli's moral outlook was Graeco-Roman, not Christian, public and
communal rather than private and individual. He did not emancipate
politics from morality so much as introduce 'a differentiation between
two incompatible ideals of life, and therefore two moralities'. One
values courage, vigour, strength, order and public achievement. The
other posits a moral universe where the ideals of charity, mercy, love of
God, forgiveness of enemies, contempt for the goods of this world and
blessed peace in the hereafter are accorded the highest evaluation. One
morality is oriented towards public life and communal happiness; the
other, towards personal life and salvation in the world to come.[49]
Berlin's Machiavelli does not formally condemn Christian morality:
the things men call good are indeed good, and words like good, bad,
honest, dishonest are used by him as they were in the common speech
of his time. He merely says that the unequivocal practice of Christian
virtues, especially on the part of rulers, makes it impossible to build a
stable, strong and prosperous society. Machiavelli is thus an incipient
moral pluralist, forcing us to choose between two sets of ends that are
equally 'moral' but mutually exclusive and irreconcilable. 'One can
save one's soul, or one can found or maintain or serve a great and
glorious state; but not always both at once.'[50]

Other commentators have already noted that Berlin's contrast of two
moralities, Christian and pagan, is somewhat simplistic; for there are
no ancient moralists, after Socrates, who would condone the kind of
behaviour Machiavelli defends in his two famous political treatises.[51]
That ancient civilization gave tangible form to his value-preferences is
undeniable: heroism and public spirit were glorified, and the other-
worldly ideals of Christianity could find little sustenance in pagan religion. Still, no Roman code of morality ever sanctioned cruelty and
deceit in the interests of political power. Machiavelli was selective in his
paganism, praising its active and aggressive side, while ridiculing those
elements that failed to tally with his vision of politics. Self-consciously
or not, he wanted to restore pagan values to their pre-philosophical,

pre-Platonic meaning. When Plato and Aristotle condemned the Spartan way of life and extolled the *vita contemplativa*, they were quarrelling with the Greek culture they had inherited. Ancient Greece has been dubbed a 'results-culture'.[52] 'Good' intentions were irrelevant, since the only important judgements that could be passed upon a man concerned the way in which he discharged his allotted social function. 'Good' for the Greeks meant 'good at' or 'good for', never good in and of itself. To us, it makes perfect sense to say that a king is 'good but not courageous or clever'. In Homeric times, this assessment would have been dismissed as an unintelligible contradiction. 'Goodness' was, by definition, equivalent to success – an equation that was firmly denied by later pagan philosophers, including Cicero.[53]

If Berlin's thesis falls down because he treats pagan morality as a monolith, Croce's contention that Machiavelli divided politics (the sphere of instrumental values) from morality (the sphere of ultimate values) is equally dubious. It would surely be odd for Machiavelli to accept the universal validity of Christian morality but nevertheless pronounce it inapplicable to such a vast area of human interaction. It makes sense to search for a more natural interpretation of his utterances. A plausible case can be made that, for him, Christian moral law no longer retained its supra-empirical necessity. Rather, empirical necessity itself became a new moral imperative, since its function was to create a certain type of good. While he was hardly a systematic moral philosopher, we find in his thought glimmers of modern consequentialist ethics, where the goodness of ends trumps the goodness of means. This would mark a significant departure from the deontological ethics of Christianity, where the goodness of an act is dependent on its conformity to universal moral rules. Virtuous behaviour is thereby separated from its results, however harmful. Machiavelli, like Bentham centuries later, wanted to define virtue in terms of consequences. Of course, he did not spell out this new moral perspective in any detail – a reticence only partly explained by his lack of aptitude for technical philosophical discourse. When he was writing, the idea of a purely rational ethic, not subject to the dictates of religion, was unheard of. The conception of 'how things ought to be' remained closely bound up with 'the eternal beyond' and the magnificent array of divine ordinances. Morality and religion were one – and even Machiavelli did not dare to question this openly. Nevertheless, it is hard to escape the impression that, in his writings, the ideal ruler of classical and Christian lore has been replaced by the means–end calculus.

Some might think it anachronistic to view Machiavelli as a founding father of utilitarianism, a quintessentially liberal philosophy, indelibly associated with nineteenth-century optimism. They would be wrong. The mentality of the English shopkeeper – which Marx thought Benthamism reflected – had its prototype in Italian urban life during the Renaissance. The habit of calculation dominated everyday relationships. Time was seen as something precious, which had to be 'spent' carefully and not 'wasted'. The word *prudente* was common, and a few writers developed a distinctively utilitarian approach to life. To a degree, they were preaching to the converted, since the Epicurean idea that pleasure is an essential ingredient of human happiness was a commonplace.[54] Machiavelli may have been inspired by Lorenzo Valla's well-known dialogue, *On Pleasure* (1433), where one speaker, representing the author, defends an ethic of utility, with all actions based on calculations of pleasure and pain. Anticipating Bentham, Valla attacked the emptiness of self-contained moral rectitude. Christian virtues such as faith, hope and charity were only means to some greater good, which Valla located in divine love as the ultimate pleasure for human beings whose immortal destiny carries them beyond the natural boundaries of the cosmos. This was a kind of 'Christian hedonism', a 'halfway house' between Church teachings and the purely rational theory of utilitarianism.[55] In its standard form, this theory can be expressed as the combination of two principles: (1) *the consequentialist principle* that the rightness, or wrongness, of an action is determined by the goodness, or badness, of the results that flow from it; and (2) *the hedonist principle* that the only thing that is good in itself is pleasure and the only thing bad in itself is pain. To interpret Machiavelli as a utilitarian, we must try to align him with these principles. Let us first consider whether (or in what way) he was a consequentialist.

Certainly, Machiavelli is forever advising rulers to calculate the practical costs and benefits of their actions. In pursuit of their goals, they must be prepared to lie, to cheat, to break treaties, to use loyal servants as scapegoats, and even to exterminate rivals. It has been argued, however, that Machiavelli's advice took the form of 'hypothetical imperatives' in the Kantian sense. With such imperatives, there is no question whether the end is morally good, but only what one must do in order to attain it: 'If you want to achieve X, it is essential that you should do Y.' Machiavelli is therefore not to be taken as necessarily approving the postulated end.[56] One can find textual evidence to support this view. Occasionally, he provides alternative courses, and, indifferent to the object we desire, supplies us with a choice of schemes and methods. When he says, for instance, that a new prince who wishes to be absolute must change everything – despoiling the rich, demolishing old cities and transporting the inhabitants to new places – he adds: 'These modes are very cruel, and enemies to every way of life, not only Christian but human; and any man whatever should flee them and wish to live in private rather than as king with so much ruin to men.' Nonetheless, he appears quite happy to provide a useful maxim for the man 'who does not wish to take this first way of the good'.[57]

This evidence is taken from the *Discourses*. In *The Prince*, as well, Machiavelli sometimes seems to adopt a conventional moral stance, just before offering 'technical' advice that contradicts it. He agrees in chapter XV that it would be 'most laudable' for a prince to possess all those qualities which are normally considered good. Likewise, in chapter XVIII, we are told that it is 'praiseworthy' for a prince to keep his word and be 'straightforward rather than crafty in his dealings'. But because these 'good' princes would be crushed in a world full of 'evil' men, Machiavelli sets out, with evident moral neutrality, to teach the satanic art of survival in unpropitious circumstances. Whether his prescriptions will be used for a good or evil purpose does not appear to figure in his calculations.[58]

While such passages support Croce's thesis, they are far from typical. More often than not Machiavelli forsakes the world of pure technique and asserts that certain courses of action are to be applauded because they promote the welfare of the community. Where the restoration of order and the safety of society are at stake, conventional vice might become political virtue, and conventional virtue might result in political ruin. In politics, it follows, we cannot draw a sharp line between moral virtue and moral vice: the two things often change place. In highlighting the irony of the political condition, Machiavelli hinted at a broader truth, which was memorably expressed by Shakespeare through the character of Friar Laurence in *Romeo and Juliet*:

> For nought so vile that on the earth doth live
> But to the earth some special good doth give;
> Nor aught so good but, strain'd from that fair use,
> Revolts from true birth, stumbling on abuse:
> Virtue itself turns vice, being misapplied,
> And vice sometime's by action dignified.
>   (Act II, Scene iii)

The prime example of this paradox – adduced by Machiavelli – is Cesare Borgia, whose ruthless methods were necessary to rid the Romagna of the plague of petty tyrants that had reduced the population to abject servitude. Borgia 'was accounted cruel; nevertheless, this cruelty of his reformed the Romagna, brought it unity, and restored order'. He must therefore be judged kinder than the Florentines who, to avoid resorting to violent and repressive measures, allowed the warring factions in Pistoia to destroy the city's peace and prosperity. Tough-minded princes, prepared to take harsh action to keep their people loyal and united, are infinitely more merciful (and, by implication, moral) than princes who, 'being too compassionate, allow disorders which lead to murder and rapine'. Disorders, Machiavelli continues, 'always harm the whole community, whereas executions ordered by a prince only affect individuals' – spoken like a true utilitarian.[59] Consider, too, the following statement: 'In the actions of all men, and especially of princes, where there is no court of appeal, one judges by the result.' By ignoring the exigencies of statecraft, the ruler who 'never preaches anything except peace and good faith' turns out to be 'an enemy of both'.[60] The same point is made in the *Discourses*, where Romulus is defended over the killing of his brother Remus. This act was necessary, Machiavelli says, so that supreme authority in founding the new state of Rome should be in one person's hands, as was essential for the success of such a venture and thus for the 'common good'. No wise person, he insists, would ever condemn a ruler for such extraordinary actions where they were beneficial to the public. Quite the reverse, for 'when the deed accuses him, the effect excuses him; and when the effect is good . . . it will always excuse the deed; for he who is violent to spoil, not he who is violent to mend, should be reproved'.[61] What Machiavelli is saying is that so-called 'dirty hands' are, in some circumstances, actually clean. That is to say, it is not necessarily 'bad to use cruelty' in pursuit of a worthy end.[62] In making his observations and recommendations, he is not tormented by a 'bad conscience'; on the contrary, he wants to abolish the very idea of 'bad conscience', with respect to political leaders at any rate.

Having established that Machiavelli was a consequentialist, we now turn to the question of whether he can plausibly be considered a hedonist who believes that pleasure is the only thing good in itself, and that all things (attributes, acts, values) we describe as 'good' are good only insofar as they maximize pleasure. Machiavelli certainly foreshadows Bentham in seeing human beings as creatures of appetite, as pleasure-seeking and pain-avoiding animals.[63] Reason, in other words, does not reign in the human soul; its function is adviser and aid to appetite and ambition. He also, like later utilitarians, seems to regard happiness (*felicità*) as the main goal of society, though he associates this not with pleasure as such (at least, not explicitly), but with order and prosperity.[64] However, Bentham, when discussing society as a whole, by and large identified pleasure with material prosperity and personal security. Satisfaction of appetites, after all, can be maximized only where such conditions obtain. *Pace* Croce, moreover, Machiavelli's attitude to traditional virtues was that of a utilitarian, not that of a Christian who reluctantly feels that these virtues, while intrinsically valuable, must sometimes be set aside when matters of state are at stake. A passage quoted above from *The Prince* stipulates that in 'the actions of all men' – not just of princes – 'one judges by the result'. The state of a man's soul, what he wills and why he wills it – these do not, and should not, influence our opinion of his worth.[65] Christian (and classical) morality enjoined not only doing the right thing, but doing it for the right reason – outward conformity to moral law was insufficient. To obtain virtue, we must wish to be, not simply appear to be, what we want others to think we are. Our motives must be pure and transparent. Machiavelli has it the other way round. It is necessary to make an outward show of conformity to conventional moral law even when one is flouting it. Outward conformity – the appearance of Christian virtue – *is* sufficient: 'To those seeing and hearing him [the prince], he should appear as a man of compassion, a man of good faith, a man of integrity, a kind and religious man.' Machiavelli adds that if the prince actually 'has these qualities and always behaves accordingly he will find them ruinous'.[66] The conclusion is obvious: *actually possessing* 'these qualities' is a hindrance to effective rulership. Machiavelli comprehensively devalues the attributes that Christians hold dear. 'Virtues' such as compassion, kindness, good faith and integrity are not good in themselves or because they enjoy divine approval; they are good only to the extent that their existence, or their *apparent* existence, contributes to the well-being of the state. They are there to be manipulated rather than cherished.

Even when Machiavelli praises the virtues of the ancient Romans – virtues he unequivocally admired – he does so in terms of the practical benefits they bring. The Romans, because of their emphasis on heroism, pride and strength (of mind and body), found it easy to defend the fatherland against external enemies who would reduce it to slavery and internal 'criminals' who would reduce it to anarchy. The warrior spirit also encouraged dynamism. The desire to conquer others could be satisfied only through the development of technology and sophisticated forms of organization. All the glorious achievements of the Romans were rooted in their militaristic and heroic value-system. Christian virtues, on the other hand, induced weakness in the face of aggression and passive indifference to the goods of this life. The Romans lit up the world with their civilization; the Christians plunged the world back into darkness.[67]

Machiavelli thought that the Roman preference for the 'man of action' over the 'contemplative man' was naturally conducive to a participative, or republican, form of government. Citizens should be public-spirited and self-assertive, not meek or abject. If enough of them lived up to this standard, dictatorial rule would be neither desirable nor necessary. It was noted earlier, during our discussion of Machiavelli's anti-utopianism, that he esteemed republicanism for the practical advantages it brought, not for its own sake or because it enabled us to realize some specific human 'essence', to live the 'good life' in a moralistic Aristotelian sense. His instrumental approach to what we might think of as absolute ideals can be further clarified if we focus on his treatment of two values that are normally associated with republicanism: the 'rule of law' and 'freedom'.

According to Viroli, 'Machiavelli regards the rule of law as the basic feature of civil and political life'; and when he speaks of the rule of law, he 'always means rule of just laws', or laws that are fair and reasonable.[68] In the opinion of Viroli's Machiavelli, a well-ordered republic 'must respect with utmost intransigence the principles of legal order'. Even if a culprit is 'the most wicked man, even if he has perpetrated the most nefarious crimes against the republic, still his legal rights must be protected'.[69] This is the way we conventionally understand the 'rule of law' – as a necessary component of justice, as an absolute value, to be preserved at all costs. But was this the way that *Machiavelli* understood the rule of law? While he certainly believed that legal procedures should be followed, except *in extremis*, he made it plain that the rule of law in this sense would not necessarily coincide with justice. Consider the chapter in the *Discourses* where he defends the practice of 'accusation', or 'denunciation' – a practice we rightly associate with totalitarian regimes. He wanted such accusations to be given a public and institutionalized form, to be incorporated within the framework of legal order. For if a citizen is 'crushed' in accordance with regular procedures, 'there follows little or no disorder in the republic, even though he has been done a wrong'. Conclusive proof of guilt would obviously not be required. The justification given for this unpleasant practice is utilitarian. In order to avoid tumult, it is 'necessary that republics give an outlet with their laws to vent the anger that the collectivity conceives against one citizen'. Another beneficial effect for the republic is that 'for fear of being accused citizens do not attempt things against the state; and when attempting them, they are crushed instantly and without respect'. So much for protecting 'legal rights'.[70] As Machiavelli said elsewhere in the *Discourses*, when one deliberates on the safety of the fatherland, 'there ought not to enter any consideration of just or unjust, merciful or cruel, praiseworthy or ignominious'.[71] For him, the antithesis of the rule of law is anarchy, not despotism. The purpose of legal procedure (what Americans call 'due process') is to provide collective security rather than justice. The rule of law, thus construed, is no moral imperative but merely a means to an end, a way of ensuring 'the greatest happiness of the greatest number', to use Bentham's famous expression.

The same can be said about Machiavelli's idea of freedom. Not being a philosopher, the Florentine Secretary never offered a systematic analysis of what he meant by 'freedom'. Given his attitude to the rule of law, it is pretty clear that his concept did not include the rights of dissident minorities or individuals who rejected commonly received principles. In his day, no one connected freedom with the right to think or say whatever you like, and Machiavelli never begged to differ. In principle, though, he favoured freedom of speech on the grounds that the best policy is likely to emerge through consideration of all available alternatives and viewpoints. By temperament, moreover, he was inclined towards an attitude of live and let live, as long as public safety was not compromised. But he was unwilling to give these preferences the status of *rights*, since he believed that, where the public is corrupted by selfishness and cowardice, unrestricted tolerance and debate is nothing short of suicidal.[72] Freedom, it follows, was for him a conditional good rather than an abstract good. But what exactly did he mean by it? Answering this question will require us to draw inferences from the scattered passages where he uses the term.

Sometimes Machiavelli talks about freedom (*libertà*) in relation to states as such, by which he means that they are beholden to no other state. 'Free' states are independent as opposed to enslaved or subordinate.[73] But he mainly uses the word 'freedom' in the sense of a 'free

way of life' – a type of freedom he literally identifies with republics.[74]
Taking all this into account, we can speculate that a 'free' people
would not be subject to the whims of foreigners, and would live under
laws to which citizens have freely given their consent. Since Machiavelli,
in one passage, contrasts 'free men' with 'those depending on others', we
can further speculate that, for him, an *individual* is free when he lives in
a free society and is dependent, not on the will of another individual, but
on the laws alone. Freedom, as Machiavelli conceives it, entails the un-
impeded pursuit of one's self-chosen ends, whatever they might be: he
does not, in Aristotelian fashion, say that we are free only when our
activities embody our deepest human purposes, for he rejects the
premise that there exists some distinctive human 'essence'. Thus, individual freedom is a matter of personal independence, constrained only
by civic responsibilities that are defined in law.[75]

According to Machiavelli, people do not value freedom for its own
sake but only 'to live secure', to pursue their own chosen ends without
fear. '[T]he common utility that is drawn from a free way of life', he
tells us, 'is being able to enjoy one's things freely, without any suspicion, not fearing for the honor of wives and that of children, not to be
afraid for oneself.'[76] He, too, adopts an instrumental attitude to freedom, seeing it as a way, in normal circumstances, to maximize the
'public utility' – a Benthamite term he employs on a number of occa-
sions. Why? We have already seen how, in his view, popular involve-
ment in the governing process – an aspect of the 'free way of life' – is
generally a recipe for good laws and political stability. Unless the
people have fallen into corrupt and servile patterns of behaviour, republican government equals good government. Machiavelli also proffered
the opinion, later to become conventional liberal wisdom, that freedom leads to material prosperity. Among his admirers on the left of
the political spectrum, a legend has grown that he was inimical to
acquisition. True, he did once say that 'the most useful thing that may
be ordered in a free way of life is that the citizens be kept poor'.[77]
Wealth can make a people soft and complacent; it offers opportunities
for financial corruption and encourages self-absorption at the expense
of the common good. Machiavelli could occasionally sound like a
socialist, though his stigmatization of private greed ostensibly
stemmed from his belief in the inevitability of war (greedy people
cannot be bothered to make sacrifices in defence of the fatherland),
and not from any idealistic love of equality. He never proposed
social reforms and never thought it necessary to keep inequalities of

purely by reference to their ability to maximize happiness), their moral judgements will usually overlap with those of deontological moralists. This would explain why Machiavelli frequently uses terms like 'good' and 'evil' in a manner acceptable to Christians. Anyone who, in his private relationships, disobeys moral conventions which have stood the test of time threatens the delicate social balance and deserves nothing but reproach.

Political life, however, is a jungle. Here a fetishistic attachment to traditional moral rules will deliver the opposite of happiness. When Machiavelli makes statements to the effect that 'all men are bad', he is really referring to man as he functions politically – in a context where the natural ties of affection and sympathy are stretched to the breaking point. The ruler who acts as if he were surrounded by his loved ones, when he is in fact surrounded by predators, will come to grief, and probably destroy the stability of his state in the process. As a guardian of the public interest, he should behave like an 'act utilitarian', who will not recoil from acts of betrayal, deceit, injustice, cruelty, or the like if these are necessary to increase or preserve 'the greatest happiness of the greatest number' in the particular situation.[79]

Both 'rule' and 'act' utilitarianism (and let us stress that these are modern terms which were never employed by Machiavelli) have the effect of bringing morality down to earth. What counts is not adherence to transcendent norms or divinely ordained purposes, but the maximization of empirically ascertainable well-being. And, of course, a preference for the observable and the concrete over the abstract and the imaginary is what lies at the core of Machiavelli's realism. Politics and ethics alike had to be located in the real world of space and time. This, to Machiavelli, was the key to human happiness. Others have disagreed. Idealists and moral absolutists cannot accept that ideals are no more than dispensable additions to the brute conditions of competitive life, that politics is merely the strategic application of force and deception, and that morality is reducible to a calculus of practical advantage. For such thinkers, Machiavelli's teachings are the path to perdition. This harsh verdict may or may not be correct. What should be beyond dispute, however, is that Machiavelli articulated a new and influential way of seeing the world. We now need to explore his legacy and reach some sort of judgement about its value.

6 • The Legacy

1. Machiavelli's genius

'The problem at the heart of intellectual history', writes Kenneth Minogue, 'arises from the fact that ideas have two aspects'. He proceeds to explain:

> they are abstract and universal, and it is in virtue of this character that they allow communication to bridge such gulfs as person to person, epoch to epoch and culture to culture. But the thinking of any idea is also a specific occurrence which has a spatio-temporal location and a social context. Philosophers are interested in the abstract ideas, historians in the individuality of the utterance, and the problem of the intellectual historian is how to negotiate this extremely interesting and poorly demarcated frontier.[1]

In recent Machiavelli scholarship, the historical contextualists have held sway, effectively dissolving his thought into the tradition of Florentine republicanism. This approach can carry with it the implication that Machiavelli belongs entirely to Renaissance Italy, and that his ideas can have no relevance at all to any other age. Contextualism, however, need not deny the continuity of human experience. As practised by John Pocock, for example, it discovers great integrative themes that transcend specific settings. In *The Machiavellian Moment*, he appears indifferent to 'spatio-temporal location', laying stress on the developmental links between Aristotle, ancient Rome, Machiavelli and even the American Revolution.[2] The substance of this 'paradigm' or tradition, we learn, is the idealization of the citizen as an active agent who transforms himself by virtue of civic engagement, thereby keeping corruption and despotism at bay. The 'context' here is not a particular time or place but a free-floating political vocabulary, defining the values and procedures of 'civic humanism'. Historical contextualism, whether it emphasizes continuity or discontinuity, tends to ignore the peculiar or distinctive characteristics of the object of study. In the case of Machiavelli, his thought is made almost to disappear in a grey mist of Aristotelian and humanist discourse. The context, however delineated, becomes not just a way of determining the meaning of his texts but a practical substitute for them. The words on the page are filtered through an interpretative framework of conventional understandings and assumptions that effectively delimits their semantic or lexical content. My own approach to Machiavelli has been very different: I have reconstructed the context of his writings in order to distinguish their innovative suggestions and observations from the ideas he shared with his predecessors and contemporaries. Of course, evidence can be interpreted in diverse ways, depending on fine judgements as to the significance of certain utterances or actions. My preference for what is 'abstract and universal' in Machiavelli, over the more fashionable contextual approach, may not correlate with any order of superior to inferior validity; it may simply be the equivalent of describing the glass of water as half-full rather than half-empty. But it can at least give us an understanding of why Machiavelli has always been enlisted in the ranks of the greatest political thinkers.

His greatness, however, does not reside in the perspicacity of his precepts or recommendations, nor in the insights of his various historical analyses. As a historian, Machiavelli was not especially penetrating. His static view of human nature, his reluctance to accept that our attitudes and perceptions may be historically transient, made him averse to structural or 'holistic' explanations, and prone to facile comparisons between Renaissance Italy and ancient Rome. He never investigated the economic and social causes of Italy's enfeeblement. Nowhere does he discuss the decline of economic dynamism brought about by guild restrictions and established privileges, and exacerbated by parochial attachments to small administrative units. Diplomatic and military incidents, instead of being regarded as symptoms of deeper processes, are elevated to the status of sufficient causes. Too often he accounts for historical events in terms of what key individuals did or did not do. While he recognized that our intentions could be thwarted by forces beyond our control, identifying these forces with *fortuna*, or chance, became a substitute for further analysis. As for Machiavelli's political rules-of-thumb, these were often of doubtful value or even contradictory. Consider his view that a republic must expand or die, 'since all things of men are in motion and . . . must either rise or fall'.[3] This analogy with a physical body moving through the air is highly misleading, for the simple reason that, in human affairs, aggressive expansion (kinetic energy) can actually hasten decline or ruin, whereas the projectile will not fall to the ground until the force propelling it (kinetic energy) has been expended. The broader problem is that Machiavelli's sweeping generalizations often fail to carry conviction. Guicciardini famously pointed out that Machiavelli's examples 'can be turned around completely'.[4] What 'works' and why it 'works' is frequently so ambiguous that the opposite tactic might have been even more successful, and the successful tactic might readily have failed. Sometimes Machiavelli acknowledges this complication and refuses to make an unqualified generalization, but at other times he seems to face in two directions at once. In chapter V of *The Prince*, for example, he tells us that 'there is no surer way of keeping possession' of a newly acquired territory – especially one that is accustomed to living in freedom – than by 'devastation'. Those in the conquered population who are not literally wiped out should be 'dispersed and scattered'.[5] In the *Discourses*, the same point is made without qualification:

> The best remedy whoever becomes prince of either a city or a state has for holding that principality is to make everything in that state anew . . . that is, to make . . . new governments, with new names, new authorities, new men; to make the rich poor, the poor rich . . . besides this, to build new cities, to take down those built, to exchange the inhabitants from one place to another; and, in sum, not to leave anything untouched in that province, so that there is no rank, no order, no state, no wealth there that he who holds it does not know it is from you.[6]

In chapter III of *The Prince*, however, Machiavelli says of newly acquired territories that it is best 'if their old ways of life are undisturbed'.[7] A later chapter (XIX) echoes this sentiment, informing us that a prince should 'avoid anything which will make him hated and despised'. This means that he should abstain from being 'rapacious and aggressive with regard to the property and the women of his subjects. He should refrain from these.'[8] So which is it? Should princes cruelly destroy the lands they have conquered, despoiling the rich, expelling or deporting whole segments of the population, abolishing established practices? Or should they leave the new territory pretty much intact and thus provide no fuel for the fires of revenge and rebellion? That the maxims Machiavelli derives from historical observation sometimes cancel one another out is particularly evident in his approach to the 'middle way', the way of moderation and caution. Even though he repeatedly states as a general principle that action should be decisive and that hesitation is fatal, he also counsels a policy of temporizing here and there throughout his works.[9] His desire to discover general rules, applicable to all situations, was often thwarted by the complexities of reality.

Because of the suspect utility of Machiavelli's *regole generali*, I have not tried the reader's patience by exploring them in detail or by analysing their historical validity. At any rate, Machiavelli's contribution to intellectual history is to be found, not in his particular recommendations to rulers, but in (what we might call) the deep conceptual structure of his thought. What made him great was the originality of his *approach*, of his analytical assumptions and categories, rather than the validity of his conclusions (though these were sometimes shrewd and perceptive). If the dominant feature of the past five centuries has been the secularization of thought, then we can say without too much exaggeration that Machiavelli ushered in the modern world. True, the spell of religious authority had been broken before he sat down to write. In humanist historiography, the idea of divine grace and providence had already disappeared as a determining force in political destinies and historical events – to be replaced by human nature, political skill and armed power as the decisive factors in the historical process. But no one, before Machiavelli, had preached the gospel of pure empiricism. He was the first prophet of a humanism that allowed man to work out, on his own, unconstrained by religion, natural law or any metaphysical limit whatsoever, the nature and parameters of the human order. The world of Dante was essentially mystical and ethical, the world of Machiavelli primarily human and logical. His case for 'real truth', as distinct from 'imaginary things', was built in opposition to the prevailing view that the universe was governed by Reason or Mind.[10] In his radical form of anti-essentialism, there are no transcendent moral truths whose validity is independent of context. Reason does not inhabit an autonomous realm; it is a purely calculating and instrumental faculty, the servant of empirical needs. The only good that human beings can attain is the earthly good of satisfying their desires for power, wealth and glory. Since reality was nothing more than a system of physical motions, devoid of inherent purpose, the Christian concentration on the afterlife was not just otiose but positively harmful.

Machiavelli's aversion to metaphysical posturing, his contempt for abstract universals, was the underlying cause of his contribution to political analysis, which can be broken down into a number of components. The *first* is his insistence that the primary subject-matter of politics is the struggle for power in all its diverse and concealed forms.

The implication is that the laws of political life cannot be discovered by an analysis which takes men's words and beliefs at their face value. Slogans, declarations, constitutions, laws, theories must be related to the whole complex of social facts in order to uncover their political and historical meaning. Machiavelli's pessimistic view of man, along with his keen appreciation of intractability, of social resistance and inertia, would seem to align him with the conservative tradition. When he laments the 'malignity' of human nature and cautions that 'in all human things . . . one inconvenience can never be suppressed without another's cropping up',[11] he strongly resembles the enemies of the Enlightenment. Like them, he was more disposed to look at things than at words, and was never drawn to mistake a cherished programme for an achieved reality. And yet, as Gramsci recognized, there was something 'essentially revolutionary' in his mindset, something profoundly uncongenial to practising conservatives in active politics and irreconcilable to the interests they seek to protect.[12] Whereas, say, Burke, in true conservative fashion, approached the state with pious awe and sentimental reverence, Machiavelli simply tore away the veil, exposing the stark nakedness of the 'emperor'. With breathtaking cynicism, he 'demystified' the sentiments and 'eternal truths' that hid the fact of universal domination. Political actions and rhetoric must be related to real life. What practical or psychological needs do they express? What will be their impact on actual behaviour? Whose interests do they serve, and why? In Machiavelli's day, people had begun to ask such questions, but there was still the tendency to study man from the perspective of the ideal rather than the real, to judge political behaviour solely with reference to a Christian code of ethics. As Machiavelli complained, there was a tremendous preoccupation with 'imaginary things', ideal republics or principalities, specifying 'how one should live'.[13] For him, in contrast, the object of study was *de facto* government and the ways in which this diverged from, or flatly contradicted, *de jure* government. He affirmed a science of politics based on the observation and analysis of what exists, of the processes and structures of power. Even when his observations were limited and his analyses defective, he always sought to discover empirical truth, not abstract normative schemes. Not without reason is he acclaimed as the founder of modern political science.

Machiavelli's realism was prescriptive as well as descriptive. Believing that politics was little more than a struggle for power, he concluded that it could be concerned only with – as Singleton put it – the *bona exteriora*, the external effects of an agent's action, rather than the *bona interiora*, the promotion of the agent's interior life.[14] This is the *second* component of Machiavelli's contribution to political thought, and it is illustrated by his treatment of religion. Christianity, we are told, taught the wrong virtues of humility, self-abnegation and other-worldliness – precisely those virtues connected with the inner goods of the soul. What was needed, instead, was a proper civic religion, one that could encourage fear and respect for authority while at the same time inculcating military valour and love of country. Religion, as Machiavelli saw it, was to be enlisted in the service of the state; it was to be judged not by the truth-value of its doctrines but by its effects on external conduct. To interpret him as a committed Christian, reluctantly making concessions to realpolitik, is to miss the significance of what he was saying. His writings constituted a radical challenge to the traditional role of religion – a point made eloquently by Sheldon Wolin:

> Machiavelli's conception of civic virtue marked an important stage in the development of modern political thought and practice, for it symbolised an end to the old alliance between statecraft and soul-craft. Henceforth it would be increasingly taken for granted that while the cultivation of souls and personalities might be a proper end of man, it did not provide the focus of political action.[15]

The 'focus of political action' was power, and power was a means of satisfying *interests*, defined in terms of reputation and material goods. This brings us to the *third* component of Machiavelli's contribution: his preference for the 'politics of resolution' over the 'politics of imposition'.[16] As we have seen, Machiavelli is routinely depicted as an idealistic republican who sees society as a naturally harmonious unit where men can realize their essentially social natures. Nothing could be further from the truth. Rejecting all forms of essentialism, he saw nature in purely descriptive terms. Human nature is to be inferred from *actual* behaviour, and the nature of society is visible in the extant patterns of human relationships. What is natural, he surmises, is not unity and sociability but conflict between the 'haves' and the 'have-nots', or between 'he who wishes to maintain' and 'he who wishes to acquire'.[17] Since 'tumult' is natural, Machiavellian takes the view that it is also beneficial where it is conducted in moderation and structured by good laws.[18] The constant need to compromise, to find a modus vivendi, to resolve disputes through mutual concessions, precludes the imposition of final solutions whose function would be to keep the republic to a perfect unity of purpose. Such unity, according to Machiavelli, is inimical to freedom, as it prescinds from the reality of human diversity. He thus redefined the political association as an arena of conflict and struggle between opposing social values and interests. In so doing, he made a radical break with past political thought and became a herald of modern liberal pluralism. Freedom, for him as for us, requires the *assertion* of private desires, not their *submergence* in some 'collective will' – and social cohesion presupposes rather than excludes the jarring effects of interest-propelled forces.

Machiavelli's demystification of politics, his reduction of its aims to the maximization of personal utility, is combined with a similar demystification in the sphere of morality. Here we have the *fourth* component of his contribution to political thought. Some commentators insist that he never wished to supplant the ordinary Christian ethic, but simply saw politics as an autonomous human activity, unburdened by any assumptions or aims of a theological or moral character.[19] Are these commentators right? Does the Christian moral law, for Machiavelli, retain its transcendent necessity, even though it may not apply to the political realm? Or does empirical necessity become a new moral imperative, since its function is to create a certain type of goodness? Is Christian morality merely being set aside in the case of politics, or is it being replaced by a different set of ideas? The present writer has opted for the latter interpretation, arguing that Machiavelli helped to pioneer a consequentialist form of morality. By and large, the thinkers of the Renaissance assumed the essential goodness of human nature and the existence of a universal system of law and order, ordained by God. Typical was the philosophy of Marsilio Ficino, for whom macrocosm and microcosm, 'world-soul and human soul, affect one another through symmetries of psychic correspondence and mutually sustain an optimistic view of man's ability to fulfil an important destiny in a cosmos divinely ordered for human ends'.[20] The mundane, the 'earthly city', was a platform for ascent to the godhead, the soul's union with all other souls joined in the highest mind. Machiavellian man, to the contrary, is an isolated atom, stripped of all transcendent 'good' qualities, and left alone on the battlefield to face the demonic forces of nature, not least the predatory instincts of his fellow human beings. The medieval conception of the goods of the soul is absent from Machiavelli's writings. He even subverted the Christian ideal of virtue, ignoring its moral connotations and including in its meaning what we refer to as 'ambition', 'drive', 'daring' and 'will to power'. We are sometimes told that Machiavelli experienced torment and 'moral nausea' when counselling the violation of Christian morality in the face of necessity.[21] This claim is hard to credit, however. Instead of appeasing revulsion and insinuating his proposals as delicately as possible, he seemed to relish the expected reaction and employed devices to heighten it. He did not sound like a man who was reluctantly transgressing natural or divine law; rather, he sounded like a man for whom such laws did not exist. For him, grand ideals and moral codes had to be reduced to practical reality and explained as responses to objective needs and power relations. He anticipated Bentham in wanting to keep all 'empty' metaphysical notions out of his view of morality. Goodness or rightness were not inherent qualities apprehended by reason or identified by revelation. Practice, as opposed to intuition or biblical authority, was central to the determination of morality.

It is difficult to exaggerate the damage done by Machiavelli's language and ideas to the discourse on virtues and vices that early modern Christians took for granted. Ordinary personal virtues – mercy, kindness, loyalty, trustworthiness – were systematically dispensed with as Machiavelli proposed theorem after theorem of a savage political calculus. But he did not advocate ruthless methods for their own sake or because he was driven by some inner satanic force, some nihilistic hatred for his fellow man, which obliterated the distinction between right and wrong. He thought that deceit and cruelty were often necessary as means to provide beneficial results – beneficial in terms not of a Christian but of a secular, consequentialist morality. This new morality was not properly developed: Machiavelli never explicitly denied that what is conventionally called 'goodness' is actually good in some sense, but he recognized that such goodness could have bad consequences, thus becoming a servant of evil and – paradoxically – vice. A ruler, Machiavelli declared, 'should never allow an evil to run loose out of respect for a good, when that good could easily be crushed by that evil'.[22] Since he also believed that 'in everything some evil is concealed', it is clear that, to him, hiding behind conventional moral constraints – in a political setting at any rate – would usually result in evil triumphant.[23] No one before Machiavelli was willing to face this paradox squarely, and to tease out its possible implications.

Mark Hulliung has written that 'the realism/idealism dichotomy has no meaning' for Machiavelli, since he 'idealized power politics'.[24] This is true up to a point; but if he 'idealized power politics', this was because the ruthless deployment of force and threats was, in his opinion, the only way to provide order and stability in a world of predators. Only a climate of personal security, guaranteed by fire and sword, could allow people to maximize their interests and therefore promote 'public utility', or the 'greatest happiness of the greatest number'. Every dictum or theory advanced by Machiavelli flows from his preference for 'real truth' over 'imaginary things', from his determination to derive normative propositions from practical circumstances. Bearing this in mind, we can see that he was neither a saintly republican idealist nor the Devil incarnate; he was a precursor of utilitarianism who rejected metaphysics and wanted to create an environment where people could satisfy their wholly natural desires for prestige and material goods. Commentators who do not share his scepticism about metaphysical truth tend to see him through the prism of their own moral absolutism, which means that they either denounce him as a nihilistic worshipper of power or laud him as a soulmate of well-meaning professors the world over – as a prophet of peace, justice, democracy and self-realization. So we end up with two antithetical versions of Machiavelli. Both are travesties of the truth and oblige their adherents to expurgate or explain away all aspects of his thought that fail to confirm their desired description. But such polarities do not exhaust the interpretative possibilities. I have argued that there is no contradiction between 'Machiavelli the republican' and 'Machiavelli the counsellor of tyrants', for each identity expresses his realism and empiricism, his ambition to bring political morality down to earth.

2. Machiavelli's progeny

My main theme has been that Machiavelli inaugurated a new way of understanding philosophy. Classical and medieval thinkers always looked at moral/political phenomena in the light of man's highest perfection, a goal that transcended particular societies or polities. Machiavelli's approach, on the other hand, divorced politics from any kind of higher purpose, implanted in us by God or nature. Thanks largely to his efforts, much modern political reflection (especially in Italy) has adopted an empirical perspective, disclaiming speculation about perfect republics or absolute justice and focusing instead on real wants and needs. The idea is to relieve human suffering, or to increase our power over nature, or to guide humankind towards a secure and materially prosperous future.

This new empiricism has generally developed in opposition to the 'naive humanitarianism' of both religious and Enlightenment thought. It is of course customary to contrast the 'age of faith' with the 'age of reason', and, in a way, the distinction is true enough since eighteenth-century writers such as Voltaire employed reason to discredit Christian dogma. But, as Carl L. Becker has argued, the *philosophes* were nearer to the Middle Ages, less emancipated from the preconceptions of medieval Christian thought, than is commonly supposed.[25] They renounced the authority of Church and Bible, but exhibited a touching faith in the authority of nature and reason. As much as any medieval scholastic, they wished to reconcile diverse and pragmatic experience with a rational pattern of the world. According to the Christian story, man had fallen from grace into sin and error, yet happily a way of atonement and salvation had been provided through the propitiatory sacrifice of God's only begotten Son. At the appointed time, the faithful would be gathered with God in the Heavenly City, 'there in perfection and felicity to dwell forever'.[26] Becker claims that the Enlightenment thinkers shared this 'messianic enterprise'[27] to the degree that they passionately wanted to purge the world of ignorance, vice and folly, and to create a new religion of humanity, based on an ideal image of nature and natural law. The universe was seen as intelligible and rational, making it possible for men to bring their ideas and their conduct into harmony with the universal moral order. Man was, in short, perfectible. The 'perfectibility of man', said Condorcet, was 'truly indefinite'. As a devotee of mathematics, Condorcet conceived perfectibility as a never-ending asymptotic approach to a mathematical limit.[28] On this conception, the world follows a logical path to the salvation of mankind. And while this salvation will come in the earthly city, it is guided – as much as the medieval version – by the transcendent and ideal structure of natural law, which, so far from being associated with the observed behaviour of physical phenomena, is an abstract conceptual universe above and outside the real one, a logical construction, dwelling in the mind of God.

According to Becker, the Enlightenment perspective was anything but modern, for the vision of man and his world as comprising a neat and efficient machine, designed by an intelligent author of the universe, has more or less faded away. What is peculiar to the modern mind, Becker points out, is the disposition to regard the truth of things as well as the things themselves as changing entities, 'points in an endless process of differentiation, of unfolding, of waste and repair'.[29] The conception of existence as a 'purposeful drama' has been replaced by the conception of existence as 'a blindly running flux of disintegrating energy'. His depiction of the modern view of man is redolent of Machiavelli's assumption that we are alone in a hostile world:

> Man is but a foundling in the cosmos, abandoned by the forces that created him. Unparented, unassisted, and undirected by omniscient or benevolent authority, he must fend for himself, and with the aid of his own limited intelligence find his way about in an indifferent universe.[30]

In recognition of 'an indifferent universe', we accept man as he is; we do not condemn him for his lost innocence or his inability to live according to some transcendent law of nature. We no longer – if we have absorbed the lessons of modernity – see life on earth as a means to a sublime end in the Heavenly City, nor do we speculate about perfection in the earthly city. We do not hide behind 'omniscient or benevolent authority', for we remain unconvinced of its existence. To the modern mind, the world may exhibit rational patterns, but these are discoverable through empirical observation, not through logic alone, still less through divine revelation.

Modernity in this sense, arguably initiated by Machiavelli, was notably developed by the philosophers of British empiricism, starting with Sir Francis Bacon (1561–1626), an admirer of the 'Florentine Secretary', who took the first steps towards elaborating an inductive logic. But if we are attempting to trace an anti-metaphysical, or Machiavellian, tradition of *political* philosophy, Thomas Hobbes (1588–1679) cannot be ignored. It might seem odd to link him to empiricism, since he was fascinated by geometry, and his account of what is involved in all reasoning applies more nearly to mathematics than to either the natural or the social sciences: 'For reason . . . is nothing but *reckoning*, that is adding and subtracting, of the consequences of general names agreed upon for the *marking* and *signifying* of our thoughts.'[31] Reason is here restricted to the making of inferences from definitions. However, as John Plamenatz points out, Hobbes did not in fact adopt the methods of the geometer but those of the economist. For, through a combination of observation and introspection, he makes assumptions about the desires and preferences of human beings and then draws conclusions about how we are likely to behave in certain situations. The geometer, in contrast, makes no assumptions about the real world.[32] Hobbes's political thought rested on an acceptance of the radical attack launched in the sixteenth century – not just by Machiavelli and Bacon but by Montaigne and others as well – on orthodox theories such as Aristotelianism or Ciceronian humanism. Hobbes rejects essentialism in all its forms. He does not speak of man's *potentialities* and their being made *actual* in society and the state; he does not take the capacities which distinguish man from other animals and seek to show how they are developed in him by communal and political life; he does not justify society or government by explaining how they help man to become what he ought to be. Nor does Hobbes, in medieval fashion, explain the social and political order as a remedy for sin or as a means to the attainment of divine purposes for man. And while the 'laws of nature' are central to his analysis, he regards them as little more than maxims of prudence or 'convenient articles of peace' – rules for commodious living whose validity does not depend on a God who intervenes in human affairs.[33] What Hobbes says about religion is basically Machiavellian, since he, too, sees it as a powerful influence in human behaviour which should be controlled by the sovereign in the interests of social peace. True, he sometimes refers to the laws of nature as commands of God, but he does not postulate any fear of God or desire to please him to explain why men should behave themselves or submit to human rulers. These references to the Almighty may have stemmed from a reluctance by Hobbes to appear 'atheistical', though his reductive materialism, which leaves no ontological space for immaterial beings or a disembodied mind, would seem to have precisely this effect. Like Machiavelli before him, he argued that there were no *real* moral properties:

> But whatsoever is the object of any man's appetite or desire, that is it which he for his part calleth *good*: and the object of his hate and aversion, *evil*; and of his contempt, *vile* and *inconsiderable*. For these words of good, evil, and contemptible, are ever used with relation to the person that useth them: there being nothing simply and absolutely so; nor any common rule of good and evil, to be taken from the nature of the objects themselves.[34]

Man, as Machiavelli and Hobbes see him, is neither a political animal in the Aristotelian sense, nor a creature marked from birth by sin and to be saved only by the grace of God. Man is not moral by nature; he is a material being programmed to maximize his personal utility, and in conditions of scarcity this will naturally lead him into conflict with other men. The purpose of government, therefore, is purely an instrumental one of allowing men to pursue their ambitions for wealth and reputation in relative safety.

When reflecting on his own method, Hobbes failed to distinguish logical relations between propositions from causal connections between events. David Hume (1711–76), another philosopher in the Machiavellian mould and in most respects a successor to Hobbes, made no such mistake. He drew a distinction between questions of logic, which are settled by tracing the logical relations of ideas, and questions of fact, which are settled by experience and inductive inferences therefrom. Logic can establish analytical propositions (for example 2 + 2 = 4) but only 'experience and observation' can yield substantive knowledge of the world.[35] Hume therefore sought to discredit the common view that absolute moral truths could be discovered through a process of deduction from first principles. He argued, instead, that morality was purely conventional, and that its content could be explained through empirical and historical analysis. The implication of this doctrine for political thought was that ideas with rationalist underpinnings, such as natural law or the social contract, had to be discarded 'as presumptuous and chimerical'.[36] Social and political institutions developed historically, in response to the exigencies of the human condition. To Hume, men were creatures of limited benevolence placed in an environment in which goods were scarce, relative to human desires. Hence – as Machiavelli and Hobbes argued before him – man's natural condition is one of conflict. To secure social peace, conventional rules concerning the stability of possessions and the keeping of contracts had emerged more or less spontaneously. Calling these 'rules of justice', Hume thought it was in everyone's interest to respect them. Thus, justice and property were artificial devices, because dependent on convention, but at the same time rooted in human need. Government was necessary because people were often too short-sighted to realize that their interests were best served by adhering to the rules of justice. In common with Machiavelli and Hobbes, Hume was less interested in who was morally entitled to rule than in who was likely to rule effectively and command the allegiance of the people. While we might have our preferences about forms of government, we should not – according to Hume – pretend that these were born of abstract principles alone.

Hume, no less than Hobbes, may have found it inconvenient to acknowledge the influence of Machiavelli, who was still regarded as evil personified in some quarters. But in his affirmations and negations he was remarkably similar to the Florentine. Both men denied that metaphysics could establish truth about the universe; both wanted to limit the province of demonstrative reasoning; both adopted a conventional view of morality and an empirical or non-essentialist view of man and government; both were pessimistic about human behaviour and saw conflict as an existential fact in 'an indifferent universe'.

All these ideas were endorsed and developed by Jeremy Bentham (1748–1832), who can also be included in the Machiavellian tradition of anti-metaphysical empiricism. That all human knowledge is ultimately based on sense experience; that reason is a purely formal or instrumental activity; that man is a pleasure-seeking and pain-avoiding creature, self-interested by nature; that there is no 'innate faculty' or 'moral sense' belonging to man in his natural state, but that moral judgements and concepts are resolvable into a form of utility; that justice is a means of obtaining security for life and property, and so of securing the greatest utility or happiness of society as a whole – these key features of his utilitarian doctrine can all be found in Machiavelli, not to mention Hobbes and Hume. Bentham tried to dissipate the idea that words like 'duty', 'obligation' and 'rights' were names of mysterious entities awaiting men's discovery and incorporation in man-made laws or social rules. Rather, they were 'fictions'. As they stood, they did not signify anything tangible, anything that we could see, hear or experience – things like commands and the infliction of pain. Such abstractions made sense only if they could be translated into practical propositions about laws and sanctions: that is, embodied in a legal code. To claim that they have a real existence, to talk, for example, of natural and imprescriptible rights, is 'rhetorical nonsense, – nonsense upon stilts'.[37] Natural law was also a fiction, since law could be understood only in terms of the commands of an identifiable sovereign backed up by the threat of sanctions. The morality of such commands, like the morality of all human conduct, was to be evaluated by its tendency to promote the happiness of those affected, not by reference to 'empty' metaphysical abstractions. The language of 'natural right' and 'natural law' was 'so much flat assertion', 'a perpetual abuse of words', having nothing to do with reason.[38] Machiavelli would have agreed with the Benthamite determination to resolve ideas into the simple elements of sense experience, and to 'demystify' abstractions that cannot be so resolved.

It is not my intention to claim that Machiavelli *directly* influenced British political philosophy, only that he pioneered a mode of thought – hostile to abstractions, realistic about human nature, modest in its expectations concerning political action – that forms an important strand in modern liberalism. Let us pursue this point a bit further. John Pocock maintains that Machiavelli and the American Founding Fathers were linked by a common devotion to Aristotelian republicanism. James Harrington (1611–77), an English republican theorist who liked to quote passages from the *Discourses*, is deemed to be a pivotal figure, largely responsible, through his acolytes, for establishing Aristotelian conceptual structures in the political culture of the eighteenth-century colonies. To Pocock, it can be shown that the American Revolution and constitution emanated from the civic humanist tradition – 'the blend of Aristotelian and Machiavellian thought concerning the *zoon politikon*', who fulfils his nature through the '*vita activa*'.[39] If my own analysis is substantially correct, it is more accurate to say that the common denominator between Machiavelli and the Founding Fathers was their scepticism about human possibilities. Listen to James Madison, writing in *The Federalist*:

> The latent causes of faction are thus sown in the nature of man . . . So strong is the propensity of mankind to fall into mutual animosities, that where no substantial occasion presents itself, the most frivolous and fanciful distinctions have been sufficient to kindle their unfriendly passions and excite their most violent conflicts . . . The inference to which we are brought is, that the *causes* of faction cannot be removed, and that relief is only to be sought in the means of controlling its *effects*.[40]

Here we have an explanation for the American constitution, with its elaborate system of checks and balances, echoing Machiavelli's fear of popular passions, along with his desire for 'mixed' constitutional arrangements. Madison justifies liberty pragmatically, as 'essential to political life'; and even writes, in Machiavellian vein, that the regulation of interests 'forms the principal task of modern legislation'.[41] To borrow Wolin's phrasing, 'statecraft' is preferred to 'soul-craft'.

The tradition of Anglo-Saxon empiricism rejected the 'heavenly perspective' described by Becker. It was a tradition singularly devoid of illusions about man's political condition and resolutely unwilling to

comments on the subject. Neither author attempted to account for morality in terms of divine will or 'right reason'. Morality, to the contrary, developed historically, through a long and slow process of elaboration, as people became more civilized and refined their selfish or aggressive impulses to suit the needs of communal life. Also like Machiavelli, Mosca suggested that morality could differ in substance from one society to another, since ethical norms were expressions of the mass consciousness, which was itself influenced by local customs, traditions and experiences.[47] Similarly, when assessing religious and political doctrines, Mosca did not bother to ask whether they were 'true' in some objective sense; the only relevant question, for him, was whether or not they were successful – and success depended on their ability 'to satisfy the needs of the human spirit', which in turn depended upon 'the requirements of time and place'.[48] It follows that Christianity is not necessarily superior to pagan or any other kind of religion. Religious precepts 'emanate from the collective moral sense that is indispensable to all human associations'. Where that sense is weak or undeveloped, or has been allowed to decay through idleness and luxury, the society in question will be barbarous and corrupt, regardless of its formal religious make-up. Conversely, where 'the collective moral sense' is strong, any faith will ensure public order and decency.[49] Machiavelli would have appreciated this relativistic approach to religion. Relativism, I would say, is what divides Machiavelli's Italian followers from the British empiricists. The latter may have despised abstraction and cast doubt on the supposedly divine origins of Christian morality, but they believed that reflection on the empirical world could deliver objective moral judgements – Hobbes's so-called 'law of nature' being a case in point. Mosca and Pareto were more sceptical about our ability to distinguish 'good' from 'bad' and more willing to reduce morality to contextual particularities.

This contempt for metaphysical explanations is what underlies their influential attempts to transform the study of human societies into an empirical science, as rigorous as the disciplines of biology or chemistry. Rightly or wrongly, both men are associated with the *fin de siècle* doctrine known as positivism, which, on a minimalist definition, is reducible to two propositions: (1) human behaviour is constrained and determined by inescapable conditions that may be understood through causal laws; and (2) the way to discover these laws is through the observational techniques used to such good effect in the physical sciences. Machiavelli can be described as an embryonic positivist, inasmuch as he saw his task as one of transforming empirical facts into theoretical precepts. He was not primarily interested in the unique political event but in laws relating events. Pareto applauded this quest for uniformities in history, noting that 'many maxims of Machiavelli' hold 'as true today as they were in his time'.[50] Those who deny this usually miss the point. While he concerned himself 'with the problem of determining what is going to happen under certain hypothetical circumstances', an eminently scientific mode of discourse, his critics assail him with 'a mass of ethical and sentimental chatter that has no scientific status whatever'.[51] As a self-appointed standard-bearer in the Machiavellian crusade against 'ethical and sentimental chatter', Pareto frequently cites his mentor with approval, complimenting him on his sage observations and scientific methods.[52]

Mosca's attitude to Machiavelli's techniques and findings was less enthusiastic. Unlike his fellow elitist, Mosca was not particularly impressed by *The Prince* – a compendium, as he saw it, of rather dubious generalities. He *was* impressed, however, by the two 'very happy intuitions' that made Machiavelli a great thinker: (1) the idea 'that the explanation of the prosperity and decadence of political organisms is to be sought in the study of events; in other words, in their past history'; and (2) the principle 'that in all peoples who have reached a certain degree of civilisation, certain general, constant tendencies are to be found; which means, in other words, that the political nature of man is more or less the same in all times and all places'. Thus, while dismissing many of his forebear's political precepts as of 'little practical value', Mosca nevertheless praised him for his courageous and revolutionary premises.[53] Where the 'Florentine Secretary' fell short was in the excessive burden of expectation he placed upon the historical method. Although he was right to seek 'the great psychological laws that function in all the large human societies', these laws can tell us little about 'the art of attaining power and holding it'. The qualities or circumstances that will lead to success or failure in the political sphere are too multifarious to be covered by general rules – a point that even Machiavelli was forced to concede on occasion.[54]

For both Mosca and Pareto, ideals were phenomena that needed to be explained scientifically, just like falling stones or earthquakes. In their refusal to take ideals at face value, they were definitely political realists in the Machiavellian mould. They shared their predecessor's low opinion of human nature as well as his assumption that elites will always rule, no matter what the constitution says. Politics is therefore about the management of power, and the job of the scientist is to reveal the processes and structures through which power is exercised. 'States are not run with prayer-books', wrote Mosca, deliberately echoing his Renaissance mentor.[55] Any ruler conducting himself solely in accordance with generally accepted moral principles is bound to fail. As Pareto puts it, such a ruler may be a 'perfect gentleman' but he is a 'no less perfect idiot'.[56] Yet the classical elitists agreed with Machiavelli that the environment of humanity is symbolically formed and ordered. Power always rests upon moral and political doctrines ('derivations' to Pareto; 'political formulas' to Mosca) that do not correspond to scientific truth. It would be mistaken, however, to dismiss these as 'mere quackeries aptly invented to trick the masses into obedience'.[57] For they answer to a profound need in man's social nature: the compulsion to seek refuge in an illusory world of absolutes. The classical elitists also denied the Enlightenment claim that humanity is capable of continuous and indefinite progress. As true heirs of Machiavelli, they argued that, deep down, the various periods of human civilization are 'very much alike'.[58] Pareto, in denying the 'myth of Progress', explicitly embraced the cyclical theory of history, using the Machiavellian imagery of 'lions' and 'foxes' to explain the successive phases. Government, as Machiavelli taught, is always by a mixture of force and fraud, but normally one or the other predominates. A regime led by 'lions' will prefer force; one led by 'foxes' will prefer fraud. The deficiencies of pure force and pure fraud as mechanisms of rule cause the two types of regime to succeed each other in infinitely repetitive cycles.[59]

The idea of utopia is therefore fatuous, not to mention dangerous. In Mosca's words, 'society will always be a wretched and disorderly affair'.[60] People will invariably be guided by passions and needs rather than some abstract, chimerical sense of 'justice'. The ineradicability of human selfishness and irrationality is precisely what renders utopian dreamers so pernicious. Should they ever gain the power to impose their vision, they would succeed only in destroying the 'natural' and time-honoured compromises that allow frail, inward-looking individuals to live in productive harmony. Instead of utopia, we would end up with a Hobbesian 'war of all against all'. To quote Mosca again, 'any political system that assumes the existence of superhuman or heroic virtues can result only in vice and corruption'.[61] Politics must be contextual, immersed in the given reality. Mosca, with Machiavelli, believes that the best we can hope for is a balanced pluralism, based on 'a multiplicity of political forces' that mutually restrain and check one another.[62] This is not to be confused with 'democracy', or rule by 'the people'. When 'political power originates from a single source', Mosca warns, it is 'liable to become oppressive'. The ruling class 'ought not to be monolithic and homogeneous', because – as Machiavelli was the first to understand – 'freedom to think, to observe, to judge men and things serenely and dispassionately' is the product of conflict and difference.[63] Sceptical as they were about 'universal truths', Mosca and Pareto thought that the triumph of a single absolute principle really amounted to the triumph of a single social force (class or group). Thus, while they never attempted to issue moral prescriptions, they broadly agreed with Machiavelli's relativistic perspective. Ethical precepts do not descend from heaven; they reflect human needs and human choices. Although Pareto did criticize utilitarianism, his quarrel was not with the basic idea of a prudential morality but with Bentham's misguided ambition to turn this morality into a scientific calculus.

While Mosca and Pareto saw themselves as classical liberals, some of their (and Machiavelli's) ideas are also associated with the 'far right', and Pareto – as is well known – welcomed the Fascist takeover in Italy. Pessimism about human nature, the relativization of morality, belief in the inevitability of elites – these are indeed defining features of fascism. But their appeal is not *confined* to that ideology, and it should surprise no one that Machiavelli has had his admirers at the opposite pole of the political spectrum. His desire to reduce the spiritual world to terra firma was of course one that he shared with Marx. Scholars almost invariably ignore the intriguing similarities between these two great thinkers, perhaps because they seem to represent antithetical ways of understanding the social order. Machiavelli's take on human behaviour and relationships expresses what Thomas Sowell calls the 'constrained' or 'tragic' vision: men are limited in knowledge, wisdom and virtue, and all social arrangements must acknowledge those limits. Hence the eternal necessity (even desirability) of coercion and hierarchy. Marx, on the other hand, exemplifies what Sowell labels the 'unconstrained vision', which is characterized by boundless optimism: psychological limitations are artefacts that are *caused by* social arrangements and therefore eradicable through social change.[64] While one tradition accepts the tragedy of the human condition, and distrusts formulas for reconstructing society, the other tends towards utopianism in its conviction that vice and folly can be eliminated – or at least greatly reduced – through the application of reason and the public expression of good will. Given his hopes for a future society where people would be motivated by self-actualization rather than self-interest, Marx apparently falls into the latter category. Communism, he wrote, would be:

> the genuine resolution of the antagonism between man and nature and between man and man; it is the true resolution of the conflict between existence and essence, objectification and self-affirmation, freedom and necessity, individual and species. It is the riddle of history solved.[65]

Such an effusion of idealism could never have flowed from the pen of Machiavelli. And yet, Marx's explanation of the past and the present, with its emphasis on conflict and domination, invoked the 'constrained vision'. Croce once professed himself 'astonished' that no one had ever thought to describe Marx as the 'Machiavelli of the proletariat'.[66] Marx, in Croce's opinion, embodied 'the best traditions of Italian political science'; not just 'the firm assertion of the principle of force, of struggle, of power', but also 'caustic opposition' to 'the so-called ideals of 1789'. Like Machiavelli, Marx dismissed 'moralistic sermons' about political rectitude or 'human rights' as so much 'idle chatter'. By disputing the gospel of bourgeois humanitarianism, by penetrating beneath appearances to identify the links between moral concepts and material interests, he tore down the abstract barriers to the proletarian conquest of power.[67]

Marx's most glittering Italian disciple, Gramsci, endorsed and expanded Croce's analysis. He, too, understood that Machiavelli's revolutionary contribution to political thought had prepared the ground for Marxism by stressing the 'conformity of means to ends'. In other words, one should not judge a political leader by his honesty or by his adherence to the 'purely formal' concepts of equity and justice, but by his political effectiveness. Does he obtain positive results, or at least manage to avoid some specific evil? For Gramsci, the central insight of Marxism – that what is 'right' or 'wrong' must be defined contextually – is derived from Machiavelli.[68] This uncompromisingly realistic approach to political morality sits oddly with Marxist utopianism. But for all their dreams of perfect harmony, Marxists display a Machiavellian sensitivity to conflicts of interest. Pre-communist society is defined by class antagonism, a struggle for scarce resources between 'haves' and 'have-nots'. Marx sees in history a Machiavellian pattern of dominance and submission. This is always the underlying

reality, regardless of surface appearances. Where he departs from
Machiavelli is in his assumption that the pattern will be ended by the
abolition of scarcity and the establishment of a classless society ('the
riddle of history solved') – a scenario that no true Machiavellian
would ever entertain. Gramsci himself betrayed some reservations
about the communist future, which he once described as 'pure
utopia', uncorroborated by empirical evidence.[69] In his eyes, the
destruction of all speculative faiths and cosmic beliefs was essential to
Marxism in its strictest form. Not all Marxists realized this, however;
and some – the orthodox kind – were combining a quasi-religious
form of reductive materialism with a teleological understanding of
history as a logical progression to the communist goal. Effectively
investing matter with covert spiritual purposes, they were, according
to Gramsci, the equivalent of older theological thinkers whom Marx
had sought to overcome. These new 'theologians', pedlars of 'pseudo-
scientific metaphysical mumbo-jumbo', had turned matter into an
'extra-historical truth', 'an abstract universal outside of time and
space', a grotesque mirror-image of Hegel's 'Spirit'.[70] Gramsci thus
argued for a socialism without metaphysical guarantees – whether
these were found in the Kantian realm of abstract truth or in the ir-
resistible force of 'History'. Marxism, so construed, is a radical form
of anti-essentialism, 'the absolute secularisation and earthliness of
thought', evoking memories of Machiavelli's challenge to medieval
cosmology.[71]

A desire to be scientific also unites Marx and Machiavelli. Both
wanted to move from the particular to the general, to interpret individual facts as instances of empirical laws or regularities. Needless to
say, all Marxists are practitioners of the historical method; they go to
history to learn the preconditions of insurrection, the mechanics of
subversion and the various permutations of revolutionary strategy.
What they cannot do, given their intrinsic social determinism, is to
endorse Machiavelli's doctrine of a fixed and immutable human
nature. Insofar as we can speak of a 'human nature', Gramsci warns,
it is nothing more than 'the totality of historically determined social
relations'. For him, this emphasis on the historical determination of
human behaviour meant that Marxism itself had to be understood as
a form of historicism, inimical to the idea of absolute and eternal
laws. Political science must therefore be conceived 'as a developing
organism', geared to our evolving needs and assumptions.[72] With this
caveat in mind, Gramsci reaches a favourable verdict on Machiavelli's

scientific achievement, for it 'represents the philosophy of the time, which tended to the organisation of absolute national monarchies – the political form which permitted and facilitated a further development of the bourgeois productive forces'. It has to be admitted, says Gramsci, that Machiavelli was not a 'pure' scientist, since his scientific efforts were guided by a passionate attachment to specific goals.[73] But Gramsci saw nothing wrong with combining empirical analysis and normative aspirations, as long as the latter originated in real, observable trends and not in the realm of wishful thinking. He saw himself engaged in just such a Machiavellian enterprise – the furtherance of political aims through the search for regularities in the apparent chaos of events. By interpreting Marxism as a form of historicism, Gramsci may have strayed from orthodoxy. Moreover – as we have seen – he may have exaggerated the impact of 'political passion' on Machiavelli's scientific analysis. Nevertheless, Machiavelli was undoubtedly a precursor of Marxism's scientific enterprise. In his ambition to correlate sets of observable facts into generalizations or uniformities, and to avoid 'vain hopes, yearning, day-dreams' when contemplating the future, he provided a model for Marxists, Gramsci included, to emulate.[74]

Machiavelli's empirical approach to political analysis was of course dictated by his hostility to metaphysics – and this in turn made him suspicious of moral absolutes, grand designs and final solutions. The world consists of imperfect human beings competing for advantage in a situation of scarcity and existential loneliness. All else is fiction. The purpose of politics is not to transform the human personality or to enforce universal moral norms; rather, it is to regulate social competition through the manipulation of myths, the establishment of regularized procedures, and – where necessary – the judicious use of force. To repeat, this is a 'constrained' or 'tragic' vision of life: human beings are intrinsically bad and cannot be relied upon to discipline their behaviour in accordance with conventional moral rules. Because social existence is precarious, the spectre of violence cannot be exorcized from our civilization. It is an ever-present reality – sometimes latent, sometimes manifest – and when it becomes manifest we must use it to destroy our enemies before they destroy us. If Machiavelli admired martial and heroic values, it is because they provided the best means of adaptation in a dangerous world. What I have tried to show is that his constrained perspective spawned a tradition of sceptical political thought, deeply opposed to the rationalistic assumptions of the

Enlightenment. But did Machiavelli go too far? Was his vision tragic, or merely odious? Even if we refuse to see him as a diabolical figure, it does not follow that his political realism is an unalloyed good.

3. The legacy assessed

Political beliefs, it has often been noted, are rooted in different conceptions of human nature. Machiavelli's fiercest critics usually adhere to a way of understanding human psychology that Steven Pinker labels the 'Blank Slate', a loose translation of the medieval Latin term *tabula rasa*, meaning 'scraped tablet'.[75] According to this theory, the human mind has no inherent structure and can be inscribed at will by society or ourselves. It follows that the differences we encounter among individuals or races or sexes come not from differences in their innate constitution but from differences in their experiences. Change the experience – change the customs or the social arrangements – and you change the way people think and act. Social inequality and social problems of all kinds are seen as remediable defects in our institutions rather than as tragedies inherent in the human condition. Because of its obvious egalitarian implications, the doctrine of the 'Blank Slate' has – in the words of Pinker – 'served as a sacred scripture' for progressive political thought.[76] Underpinning the 'unconstrained vision' of society, it was manifest in the Enlightenment notion of human perfectibility and in Marx's reduction of human nature to the ensemble of social relations. More recently, it has received expression in the 'postmodernist' belief that there is no such thing as human nature, only the floating world of our own constructions.

The idea that human nature is immutable represents the foundation of the whole Machiavellian doctrine of the eternal recurrence of typical events and of the possible renewal of historical situations through imitation of typical political accomplishments. In dismissing the possibility that human behaviour can be critically shaped by social and historical circumstances, Machiavelli no doubt exceeded the bounds of reason. But this hardly means that the opposite extreme is correct. Belief in the infinite malleability of the human psyche, the conviction that humanity can be 'restructured' at will, is contradicted by both common sense and the failed communist experiments of the twentieth century. Attempts to maintain a division between the 'Blank Slate' given by biology, and the contents inscribed by experience and culture, have been further undermined by recent developments in the sciences of mind, brain and evolution.[77] Cognitive scientists have shown that universal mental mechanisms can underlie superficial divergences across cultures (for example, Chomsky's finding that the generative grammars of individual languages are variations on a single pattern); neuroscience has demonstrated that all our thoughts and feelings depend on physiological events in the tissues of the brain (for example, convicted murderers are likely to have a smaller and less active pre-frontal cortex, the part of the brain that inhibits impulses); and evolutionary psychology has explained the traits we see in human beings as adaptive mechanisms that allowed our ancestors to survive, find mates and reproduce – which means that the rudiments of our mental life are largely a product of natural selection, not transient social conditioning.

The 'Blank Slate' is often accompanied by another doctrine which has also attained a quasi-sacred status in the modern intellectual consciousness. This is the idea, associated with Rousseau, that humans in their natural state are selfless, compassionate, cooperative and peaceable, and that blights such as greed and violence are the products of civilization. Pinker calls this the doctrine of the 'Noble Savage', which directly contradicts the view advanced by Machiavelli, and later Hobbes, that man is naturally selfish and predatory, and unable to enjoy an orderly existence in the absence of state coercion.[78] For believers in the 'Noble Savage', a happy society is our birthright, and the whole panoply of 'civilized' institutions, by corrupting our natural instincts, has made us desperately miserable.

Pinker points out that in the past two decades anthropologists have actually gathered data on life and death in pre-state societies, 'rather than accepting the warm and fuzzy stereotypes' or resting content with vague impressions inspired by gross sentimentality. What they found, in a nutshell, was that Hobbes was right and Rousseau wrong:

> To begin with, the stories of tribes out there somewhere who have never heard of violence turn out to be urban legends. Margaret Mead's descriptions of peace-loving New Guineans and sexually nonchalant Samoans were based on perfunctory research and turned out to be almost perversely wrong. As the anthropologist Derek Freeman later documented, Samoans may beat or kill their daughters if they are not virgins on their wedding night, a young man who cannot woo a virgin may rape one to extort her into eloping, and the family of a cuckolded husband may attack and kill the adulterer. The Kung San of the Kalahari Desert had been described by Elizabeth Marshall Thomas as 'the harmless people' in a book

with that title. But as soon as anthropologists camped out long enough to accumulate data, they discovered that the Kung San have a murder rate higher than that of American inner cities. They learned as well that a group of the San had recently avenged a murder by sneaking in to the killer's group and executing every man, woman and child as they slept.[79]

Researchers have also discovered that pre-state societies are spectacularly warlike. The archaeologist Lawrence Keeley has examined the proportion of male deaths caused by war in a number of societies for which data are available. His findings indicate that the figures for the indigenous peoples in South America and New Guinea are between ten and sixty times higher than those for the USA and Europe during the twentieth century, a period encompassing two world wars.[80] These statistics corroborate Freud's argument that western civilization does not *create* our nasty propensities and instincts; instead, it represses or sublimates them.

The evidence would seem to show that Machiavelli was more right than wrong when he assumed that greed and aggression were deeply rooted in human psychology. But, together with their vicious and brutish traits, all people display a host of kinder, gentler ones: compassion, love, loyalty. Although Machiavelli obviously recognized this, he did not really understand that conflict resolution must engage both sets of characteristics or motives. This myopia, this failure to consider human nature in the round, accounts for the incoherence of Machiavellianism as conventionally understood. For example, Machiavelli dedicated himself to undermining the myths – religious and political – that, by his own reckoning, were necessary to the orderly and effective functioning of society. His postulates of brute power and human corruption provided poor foundations for his desired republic. True, he performed a valuable service by reminding us that politics is a matter of reducing or managing 'inconvenience', not of eliminating it.[81] Political action typically involves accepting the lesser of two evils.[82] Pretending otherwise, searching for 'ideal' solutions, rigidly clinging to moral absolutes, will often lead to a multiplication of evils since it prevents viable and beneficial trade-offs. This is the paradox of politics: good often results in evil and vice versa. History has confirmed Machiavelli's belief that regimes and statesmen must be judged not by their expressed intentions but by the fruits of their policies. After all, noble intentions, when aligned with power, brought us the Inquisition, the Jacobin Terror in France and the

Soviet Gulags. On the other hand, no one, apart from a dedicated paci-
fist, would now deny that deviations from strict moral standards can
be justified in certain circumstances.

There are times when harsh measures, even warlike measures, are
necessary means to a higher good, or to the avoidance of some unacceptable bad. The imperfections of the human species mean that
politicians and statesmen cannot altogether avoid the infliction of
pain, or the issuing of threats that may insult the delicate sensibilities
of idealists. That said, excessive cynicism can be just as dangerous as
excessive idealism. By deriding the language of conventional morality,
Machiavelli reduced politics to a mechanism of interest aggregation and
protection, whose legitimacy will always be contingent upon the attainment of its utilitarian goals. This is a recipe for instability. Loyalty to the
state, a feeling of civic responsibility, cannot be constructed from the
raw materials of distrust and self-interest. Pervasive cynicism is incompatible with a healthy political order. As we have seen, Machiavelli was
a kind of utilitarian. For him, goodness or rightness were not intrinsic
qualities perceived by reason or specified by revelation; they were determined empirically through calculation of consequences. Ruthless
methods, so far from being desirable for their own sake, were sometimes necessary to produce optimal results. But his understanding of
the utilitarian 'calculus' was too narrow. He ignored the relationship
between the act performed and the character of the agent. Cheating,
lying, cruelty, treachery – these can have beneficial consequences in the
short run, but they have a coarsening and corrupting effect on human
character which must be incorporated into our utilitarian calculations.
And what about the demoralizing effects on the wider population?
Machiavellianism can be seen as a self-fulfilling prophecy, insofar as it
creates the feelings of alienation and mistrust that it was designed to
address. Machiavelli himself seemed to worry about this, claiming in
The Prince, for example, that a ruler should strive to maintain a reputation for honour and justice.[83] Clearly, sustaining such an image would
impose limitations on his Machiavellianism, for he would be constrained to pay more than ritual obeisance to traditional morality, and
to treat his subjects (or fellow citizens) with respect. This might, in any
case, be the way to get the best out of them. There is a slight ambiguity in what Machiavelli says about human nature. Does he view men as
naturally savage? Or just weak and frail in the presence of temptation?
If the latter, then there is a capacity for spiritual growth. A climate of
trust – one where cruelty and deceit are frowned upon – could cultivate

our more noble characteristics, making us less unruly, less perfidious. That is to say, eschewing Machiavellian policies might be the best way of rendering them unnecessary. Trust is essential to the smooth running of society, as it is both cause and effect of 'social capital', the capacity to control transaction costs through the 'soft' regulation of norms and mutual expectations rather than through hard legal rules.[84] Although Machiavelli occasionally caught a glimpse of this truth, he failed to appreciate its significance or to grasp how his own recommendations could destabilize society by destroying trust.

It would be instructive to project these issues on to a larger canvas. In both the theory and practice of international relations, realism – inspired by Machiavelli and Hobbes – is very much in evidence as a guiding principle. In its pure form, this approach assumes that there is no underlying harmony of interests among states, and that international rules and institutions merely reflect the interests of the powerful. Moral law is either reduced to expediency or deemed irrelevant in a world where predators lurk round every corner. Having demystified and dismissed all international ideals, the realist insists that the sole guide to foreign policy should be national interest, not lofty doctrines or beliefs. He generally has a low opinion of human nature, assuming that people are more inclined to do evil than to do good. This implies that conflict is normal, as is the use of force – a perfectly rational activity from the standpoint of those who anticipate gain to themselves or their nations. Since there is no ultimate global authority possessing the requisite power to enforce compliance with rules of conduct, security comes from economic and military strength, reinforced by strategic alliances with other states. According to this perspective, then, international relations take place in a competitive and hostile environment where there are winners and losers. In order to avoid (unwanted) wars and – worse – losing, attention must be paid to the 'balance of power': potential aggressors must know that the costs of any hostile actions will be prohibitive. *Raison d'état* is central and dictates what a state must do.

It is a moot point whether practitioners of realism in the international arena are motivated by knowledge of Machiavelli or simply use his ideas as a retrospective justification for actions they would have undertaken anyhow. Whatever the case, realism is not the only or the 'natural' approach to international relations, at least not *in principle*. There is a contrary tradition, originating in Christian universalism and later developed by the philosopher Immanuel Kant (1724–1804). The 'idealist' perspective posits that there are certain ethical principles binding on all international actors. Expediency and the pursuit of naked interest are frowned upon. Behaviour should instead be motivated by ideals, higher laws, or natural and universal rights, which are independent of human artifice. The tradition is cosmopolitan inasmuch as it elevates our common humanity above the national unit. Because the ultimate ideal is a universal global order, great emphasis is placed on international law and transnational institutions. Whereas realists are pessimistic about human nature, idealists are optimistic and stress our capacity for virtue and rationality. Accordingly, international relations should proceed through persuasion and dialogue rather than threats or force, which are deemed to be counter-productive. Given the naturally peaceable instincts of human beings, conflict is not normal but aberrant. War typically results from a failure of understanding, whether caused by lack of communication or by emotions overriding judgement. For the idealist, in consequence, the cure for war is better communication between potential enemies as well as a de-emphasis on the very things which the realist believes will *prevent* war: namely, patriotism and military might.[85]

It is easy for a Machiavellian realist to poke holes in the idealist position. The latter champions universal principles of morality, but do such principles exist? If they do, there is very little international agreement about their content except at the most abstract level. Everyone, it is fair to say, would concede that killing another human being without proper justification is wrong. What counts as proper justification, however, is a matter of great and apparently irresolvable controversy. Similarly, everyone can probably agree on a minimal list of 'human rights', assuming they are abstractly defined. But there is no international consensus on what such rights mean in practical terms, or (even) on whether they are truly 'natural', as opposed to being historically contingent constructs of western provenance. Abstract principles are also notorious for conflicting with one another in any given context. For example, it appears that in the case of Kosovo the principle of never waging an aggressive war on a sovereign state came into contradiction with the principle of protecting human rights. Abstract principles must be translated to apply to specific situations, and this is where diverse value-systems and cultural traditions will come into play. The 'international community' is not a moral community in any real sense. This is not necessarily a bad thing, from a realist perspective. Must we all see ourselves as part of a community of mankind? And is not the idea of a 'common humanity' simply code for the global imposition of western values? While national boundaries may be artificial, their historical longevity has established what most people would regard as morally relevant distinctions. Are my obligations to foreigners living in alien cultures identical to my obligations to my fellow citizens? It would seem perverse to answer in the affirmative. Paradoxically, the realist could add, cosmopolitan moralism is more likely to increase than to reduce international conflict. Given the expense and risks of war, ruthless calculations of national interest would rule it out in many situations where abstract moralism, unconstrained by expediency or doubt, would justify or even require it. Alternatively, the idealist approach could have the opposite effect. Confronted by aggression, the moralist might seek peace at any price, thus allowing bullies to prey on the weak with impunity. Whether it leads to misplaced pacifism or 'humanitarian' aggression, idealism, in the realist analysis, will have a disastrous effect on the peace and safety of the world.

These powerful arguments suggest that a Machiavellian approach to foreign affairs *could be*, in effect, more compassionate than an overtly compassionate mode of proceeding. Realism, however, is not without its own defects and contradictions. As suggested earlier, the conviction that one cannot trust one's neighbours is likely to become a self-fulfilling prophecy, as it discourages cooperation and therefore generates further suspicion. Pure expediency as a general principle of action would ultimately be self-defeating: no one would know where they stood; friends could become enemies and enemies friends, depending upon the relative advantages to be gained by adopting such a stance. Peace would be fragile at best. There would be no loyalty or continuity, and long-term strategies would be futile. Of course, few if any countries are able to follow a policy of pure expediency in their external relations. The pursuit of national interest is limited by strategic alliances, historic relationships, public expectations and the conventions of international law. But this simply points to the limitations of Machiavellian realism. Despite the absence of a world government able to enforce its will, states do not and cannot assume that they are operating in a Hobbesian state of nature. While there may be no international *community* in any meaningful sense, there *is* something approaching an international *society*, loosely regulated by acknowledged rules and institutions, and striving to increase the areas of interstate cooperation.[86] Although realism may be appropriate in this context, it would be a modified realism, incorporating some of the insights of the idealist model. When Machiavelli complains, as he sometimes does, that politicians are too 'humane' to take the harsh and violent measures that are often necessary, he forgets that such measures – the equivalent of military aggression in the international sphere – can make a bad situation worse by diminishing political capital and setting off an unpredictable chain of events. 'Machiavellian' has become a byword for subtlety, but subtlety is what is lacking in the methods associated with that label.

Nevertheless, I would argue that the overall impact of Machiavelli's revolutionary transformation of political thought has been more benign than malignant. While *undiluted* realism may be harmful and absurd (even unrealistic), in modified form it offers valuable insights and suggestions to politicians and political analysts alike. The modern science of politics begins with Machiavelli and his understanding that things are not always what they seem. Moreover, it is his realism that links him to modern liberal democracy. Commentators tend to fight shy of this conclusion. Those who wish to defend his democratic credentials feel obliged to exaggerate his egalitarian and liberal inclinations and to bury his 'bad' side beneath a pile of sophistry. These 'gentle Machiavellians'[87] are the antithesis of those who see Machiavelli as the epitome of evil, as a kind of devil who – in the words of Leo Strauss – encouraged 'a movement from excellence to vileness' and instigated a 'stupendous contraction' of our moral horizon.[88] Hulliung is less moralistic but he concurs that Machiavelli was an anti-humanist whose 'heroic and violent values' are 'quite incompatible with modern liberalism, the ideology of tolerance, pluralism, and compromise'.[89] But we have already seen how Machiavelli *anticipated* many of the ideas of 'modern liberalism', including the ones listed by Hulliung. What makes the Italian a forerunner of liberal democracy is not (as some would have it) an idealistic attachment to popular participation but precisely the commitment to 'power politics' that Hulliung thinks distinguishes him from us. The core assumption of realism – that politics is essentially about the distribution of power – underlies the western concept of democracy, though we are loath to admit it. Let me elaborate.

The Italian thinker Norberto Bobbio has made a useful distinction between two types of political realism. One, resting upon the counterposition of 'real' and 'ideal', scorns utopian escapism, ridicules the search for human perfection or final solutions; the other, based upon the counterposition of 'real' and 'apparent', unmasks the hidden aspects of power, demystifies the status quo.[90] Machiavelli was of course a realist in both senses. Idealism repelled him. The point of political activity was not to fulfil some distinctive human 'essence', or to pursue some ultimate moral principle, or to prepare human beings for their eternal destiny. Machiavelli's state is morally neutral. While he held clear views about the appropriate behaviour of citizens and subjects, he never tried to explain or justify the state as the condition of their improvement, still less their perfection. It exists simply to enforce the ground rules in the existential conflict between competing values and interests, and to create an environment that is conducive to the maximization of human preferences. As such, it is worthy of our esteem and affection, but it has no purposes beyond those assigned to it by its citizens or rulers. This is basically a modern liberal view of the state. While Strauss may denounce the 'stupendous contraction' of our moral perspective, it is worth pointing out that the most destructive regimes in history have been those of men who have elevated their preferences to the pinnacle of moral imperatives and who have then confidently proceeded to impose those imperatives on others. Given the diversity of modern society, the neutrality of the state, allowing for 'a pluralism of social spaces regulated by contingent and flexible criteria', seems more necessary than ever.[91] The Aristotelian idea of a 'holistic' democracy, where participation is an expression of social solidarity and shared aspirations, is increasingly looking like a casualty of modernity. The 'deconstruction' of abstract social schemes, recognition of the limited purposes of government – these are valuable Machiavellian contributions to the theory and practice of democracy. They are not to everyone's taste, however. The dominant orthodoxy of modern political philosophy assumes that the organizational principles of the good society can be defined universally, as if underlying social needs or historical patterns of behaviour were irrelevant; hence the preoccupation with abstract conceptions of 'justice' or 'rights' or 'human needs'. Within narrow academic circles at any rate, the 'heavenly perspective' manages to linger on, albeit in attenuated form. A Machiavellian approach to political philosophy would of course be much more sensitive to context and to the plurality of human aspirations.

The second aspect of Machiavelli's realism – the counterposition of 'real' and 'apparent' – can also be seen as a vital ingredient of modern democracy. To the realist, political rhetoric and rationalizations should never be taken at face value. Our rulers will invoke the 'common good' or the 'will of the people', but conflicts of interest are the

Notes

1 The Many Faces of Machiavelli

1 C. Cruise O'Brien, 'The ferocious wisdom of Machiavelli', in *The Suspecting Glance* (London: Faber and Faber, 1972), p. 16.
2 S. Anglo, *Machiavelli: A Dissection* (London: Paladin, 1971), p. 12.
3 For a definitive study of Italian diplomatic practice in the fifteenth century, see G. Mattingly, *Renaissance Diplomacy* (London: Cape, 1955).
4 Anglo, *Machiavelli*, pp. 29–38.
5 Ibid., p. 27. See, also, R. Black, 'Machiavelli, servant of the Florentine Republic', in G. Bock, Q. Skinner and M. Viroli (eds), *Machiavelli and Republicanism* (Cambridge: Cambridge University Press, 1990).
6 Anglo, *Machiavelli*, p. 142.
7 E. Cassirer, *The Myth of the State* (New Haven, Conn.: Yale University Press, 1946), p. 117.
8 See M. Praz, 'Machiavelli and the Elizabethans', *Proceedings of the British Academy*, 13 (1928), 49–97. John F. Danby has tried to explain the Elizabethan fixation on Machiavelli as stemming from the suspicion that he had stumbled upon a political truth – the unbridgeable chasm between the Christian ideal and the realities of politics. Yet this 'truth' had to be resisted, since its acceptance could lead straight to the abyss: 'There is a new sense of the fissuring of man, of a gap between the external and the internal, a possible dichotomy between the social and the spiritual. We can see it even in Hooker's contradiction: man must be thought of as a reasonable creature if we are to justify the unity of law and love, yet for reasons of government it is best to think of him as a law-breaking beast. The new element is not merely the thought of appalling wickedness. It is rather the uneasy feeling that 'wickedness' might be a social advantage. What is morally wrong might be socially expedient, a strong ruler who is bad better than a holy King who is also weak. "Pity, love and fear" may be governmental handicaps . . . Yet they are the ideal for man, and living together on any other terms than on an assumption of unifying kindness is scarcely reasonable. This honest enigma underlies everything else in the Machiavel-figure. It provides the sober basis for what would otherwise be flesh-creeping pantomime. If pity, love, and fear have become socially irrelevant, then are they true, or do greybeards merely say

they are divine? If they are not true, then the whole façade of society is a mask . . . Behind the mask there is not an angel but a devil – and notwithstanding a more reliable and efficient regulator of *Res Publica*. This man, aware of how things really work, aware of the mockery of moral claims, aware of what men really are motivated by as opposed to what they pretend to themselves, will kill the King.' The possibility of Machiavelli being right made it all the more necessary to condemn him. As a modern psychologist might say, the Elizabethans were 'in denial' and could maintain their psychic equilibrium only by denouncing the bringer of bad tidings (J. F. Danby, *Shakespeare's Doctrine of Nature: A Study of King Lear* (London: Faber, 1961), pp. 61–2).

⁹ J. J. Rousseau, *The Social Contract and Discourses*, trans. G. D. H. Cole (London: J. M. Dent & Sons, 1966), p. 59.

¹⁰ N. Machiavelli, *The Prince*, trans. G. Bull (Harmondsworth: Penguin, 1975), ch. XXVI, pp. 134–5. There are a number of English translations of *The Prince*. Since the chapters of the work are very brief – three pages or so on average – readers using other translations will be able to follow my references by consulting the relevant chapters.

¹¹ Cassirer, *The Myth of the State*, pp. 153–6.

¹² B. Croce, *Elementi di politica* (Bari: Laterza, 1925), pp. 59–67.

¹³ C. S. Singleton, 'The perspective of art', *The Kenyon Review*, XV (1953), 169–89.

¹⁴ Ibid., 180.

¹⁵ A. Gramsci, *Quaderni del carcere*, vol. III, ed. V. Gerratana (Turin: Einaudi, 1975), pp. 1555, 1572, 1601.

¹⁶ H. Butterfield, *The Statecraft of Machiavelli* (London: G. Bell and Sons, 1940), p. 57.

¹⁷ M. Viroli, *Machiavelli* (Oxford: Oxford University Press, 1998), p. 3.

¹⁸ M. Viroli, 'Machiavelli and the republican idea of politics', in Bock et al. (eds), *Machiavelli and Republicanism*, p. 144.

¹⁹ Q. Skinner, 'Machiavelli's *Discorsi* and the pre-humanist origins of republican ideas', in Bock et al. (eds), *Machiavelli and Republicanism*, p. 141.

²⁰ J. G. A. Pocock, *The Machiavellian Moment: Florentine Political Thought and the Atlantic Republican Tradition* (Princeton: Princeton University Press, 1975), pp. 40, 184.

²¹ B. Fontana, *Hegemony and Power: On the Relation between Gramsci and Machiavelli* (Minneapolis: University of Minnesota Press, 1993), pp. 72, 75, 106, 114, 125, 161, 162.

²² H. C. Mansfield, *Machiavelli's Virtue* (Chicago: University of Chicago Press, 1998), pp. 177, ix, 257.

²³ L. Strauss, *Thoughts on Machiavelli* (Chicago: University of Chicago Press, 1958), pp. 9–12.

24 M. Hulliung, *Citizen Machiavelli* (Princeton: Princeton University Press, 1983), p. 255.

25 Ibid., pp. 227–8, 237, 245.

26 *The Prince*, ch. IX, pp. 69–70.

27 N. Machiavelli, *Discourses on Livy*, trans. H. C. Mansfield and N. Tarcov (Chicago: University of Chicago Press, 1996), bk. II, ch. 2, p. 130. Hereafter *Discourses*.

28 *Discourses*, bk. I, ch. 58, p. 117.

29 J. H. Geerken, 'Machiavelli studies since 1969', *Journal of the History of Ideas*, 37 (1976), 357. This chronology, however, is not universally accepted. For a useful summary of the controversy surrounding the dating of *The Prince* and the *Discourses*, see E. Cochrane, 'Machiavelli: 1940–60', *Journal of Modern History*, 33 (1961), 133–6. As Cochrane observes, the whole debate eventually became a 'great bore' (135), whose main purpose, it seemed, was to display the subtle dialectical and philological skills of the various protagonists.

30 J. R. Hale (ed. and trans.), *The Literary Works of Machiavelli* (Oxford: Oxford University Press, 1961), p. 140.

31 *Discourses*, bk. I, ch. 9, p. 29; bk. I, chs. 16–18, 34.

32 Butterfield, *The Statecraft of Machiavelli*, pp. 54–5.

33 *Discourses*, bk. III, ch. 41, p. 301.

34 Maurice Merleau-Ponty points out that Marx always preferred 'reactionary' thinkers who recognized class struggle and the clash of opposing forces to 'progressive' thinkers who assumed that rational discussion and 'enlightenment' would turn the world into one big happy family. 'Machiavelli is worth more than Kant' fairly sums up Marx's attitude, according to Merleau-Ponty (M. Merleau-Ponty, *Humanism and Terror*, trans. J. O'Neill (Boston: Beacon Press, 1969), p. 104).

2 Setting the Context

1 J. Burckhardt, *The Civilization of the Renaissance in Italy* (2 vols), trans. S. G. C. Middlemore (New York: Harper & Row, 1958). First published in 1860.

2 For an interesting contribution to the debate, and a concise statement of the various positions, see F. Chabod, *Machiavelli and the Renaissance*, trans. D. Moore (New York: Harper & Row, 1958), ch. 4.

3 H. Baron, 'Towards a more positive evaluation of the fifteenth-century Renaissance', *Journal of the History of Ideas*, IV (1943), 48. It is worth noting that the scholars and writers associated with the Renaissance themselves spoke of the revival or rebirth of the arts and of learning that was accomplished in their own time after a long period of decay. Even if we

were convinced that this was an empty claim, we would be forced to admit that the term 'Renaissance' was not merely an invention of enthusiastic historians such as Burckhardt; it had a subjective meaning for the people of that period. See W. K. Ferguson, 'Humanistic views of the Renaissance', *American Historical Review*, XLV (1939–40), 1–28.

4   J. H. Plumb, *The Italian Renaissance* (New York: American Heritage Library, 1989), p. 9.

5   The degree of urbanization can be taken as an index of Italy's economic development. According to statistics recorded in 1338, four of the five most populous cities in Europe (Florence, Venice, Milan, Naples) were Italian (G. A. Brucker, *Renaissance Florence* (New York: John Wiley & Sons, 1969), p. 51).

6   Plumb, *The Italian Renaissance*, pp. 21–2.

7   G. Mattingly, *Renaissance Diplomacy* (London: Cape, 1955), p. 89.

8   Burckhardt, while admitting that some of the most zealous apostles of humanism were men of strictest piety, claims that the movement was generally pagan. It is likely, he tells us, that most humanists 'wavered inwardly between incredulity and a remnant of the faith in which they were brought up, and outwardly held for prudential reasons to the Church' (*The Civilization of the Renaissance in Italy*, vol. 2, pp. 479–80). Perhaps, though, the tendency in modern scholarship is to stress their piety (however questionable its orthodoxy). See D. Hay, *The Italian Renaissance in its Historical Background* (Cambridge: Cambridge University Press, 1977), pp. 181–3.

9   P. O. Kristeller, *Renaissance Thought: The Classic, Scholastic, and Humanist Strains* (New York: Harper & Row, 1961), p. 10.

10 P. Johnson, *The Renaissance: A Short History* (New York: Modern Library, 2000), p. 38.

11 E. Garin, *Italian Humanism: Philosophy and Civic Life in the Renaissance*, trans. P. Munz (Westport, Conn.: Greenwood, 1975), pp. 3–10.

12 Ibid., p. 13.

13 P. O. Kristeller, 'The philosophy of Man in the Italian Renaissance', *Italica*, XXIV (1947), 100–1.

14 P. Burke, *The Italian Renaissance: Culture and Society in Italy* (Cambridge: Polity Press, 1986), p. 198.

15 Burckhardt, *The Civilization of the Renaissance in Italy*, vol. 1, pp. 143–4.

16 J. Hankins, 'Humanism and the origins of modern political thought', in J. Kraye (ed.), *The Cambridge Companion to Renaissance Humanism* (Cambridge and New York: Cambridge University Press, 1996), p. 123.

17 Brucker, *Renaissance Florence*, p. 238.

18 Burckhardt, *The Civilization of the Renaissance in Italy*, vol. 2, p. 324.

19 Burke, *The Italian Renaissance*, pp. 195–6.

20 The literature on Italian Renaissance art is vast. I have found the following

works particularly valuable: P. and L. Murray, *The Art of the Renaissance* (London: Thames and Hudson, 1963); C. Avery, *Florentine Renaissance Sculpture* (London: John Murray, 1970); and Johnson, *The Renaissance*, pts 3–5.

21 Hay, *The Italian Renaissance*, ch. 5.

22 P. Pompanazzi, 'On the immortality of the soul', in E. Cassirer, P. O. Kristeller and J. H. Randall Jr. (eds), *The Renaissance Philosophy of Man: Selections in Translation* (Chicago, 1948), pp. 377–81. It should be pointed out that not all Renaissance philosophers asserted the supremacy of the active life. While accepting the humanist theme of the glory of man, Marsilio Ficino (1433–99), the leading Florentine Platonist, argued that the basic purpose of human life is the inward experience of contemplation, consisting in the gradual ascent of the soul towards union with God. Despite his thorough humanist education, Ficino never abandoned the heritage of medieval mysticism and was scornful of humanism's polemical attitude towards scholastic philosophy. Scholars such as Paul Oskar Kristeller have warned us against exaggerating the influence of humanism – essentially a cultural and literary movement bound by its classical and rhetorical interests – on academic philosophy during the Renaissance. Within its university redoubt, scholasticism continued to thrive. See, for example, Kristeller, *Renaissance Thought*, p. 113. For brief but useful discussions of Ficino and Pompanazzi, see Kristeller's classic article, 'The philosophy of Man in the Italian Renaissance', as well as B. P. Copenhaver and C. B. Schmitt, *Renaissance Philosophy* (Oxford and New York: Oxford University Press, 1992), pp. 103–12, 143–63.

23 Hankins, 'Humanism and the origins of modern political thought', pp. 124–33. Ironically, the republic Bruni served was far from democratic. As Brucker has pointed out, the 'patrician regimes of the *Quattrocento*' managed to '"tranquillise" politics', progressively contracting the size of the electorate and turning citizens into subjects, 'passive onlookers instead of active participants' (*Renaissance Florence*, p. 170).

24 Johnson, *The Renaissance*, p. 40.

25 Hankins, 'Humanism and the origins of modern political thought', p. 125.

26 M. Hulliung, *Citizen Machiavelli* (Princeton: Princeton University Press, 1983), p. 19.

27 Burke, *The Italian Renaissance*, pp. 193–94.

28 F. Gilbert, *Machiavelli and Guicciardini* (Princeton: Princeton University Press, 1965), p. 129.

29 F. Guicciardini, *Dialogo e discorsi del reggimento di Firenze*, ed. R. Palmarocchi (Bari: Laterza, 1932), p. 222.

3   Hostility to Metaphysics

1   A. H. Gilbert, *Machiavelli's 'Prince' and its Forerunners: 'The Prince' as a Typical Book de regimine principium* (Durham, NC: Duke University Press, 1938)

2   F. Gilbert, 'The humanist concept of the prince and "The Prince" of Machiavelli', *The Journal of Modern History*, XI (1939), 449–83.

3   Ibid., 459–60.

4   Ibid., 460–1.

5   Ibid., 462–8.

6   Nevertheless, Machiavelli was careful to exclude what Christians would regard as morally wicked behaviour from his ideal of *virtù*. In chapter VIII of *The Prince*, which considers the case of Agathocles, the tyrant of Syracuse, Machiavelli writes that 'to kill fellow citizens, to betray friends, to be treacherous, pitiless, irreligious' cannot deserve the name of *virtù*. And yet in Agathocles – the embodiment of such 'brutal cruelty and inhumanity' – he did detect a real *virtù* and greatness of spirit, an ability to confront and survive danger, to endure and overcome adversity. The Sicilian's crimes did not *constitute virtù*, but they did in a way *arise out of virtù*, since it was inconceivable that a timid or fearful man would have ever committed them (N. Machiavelli, *The Prince*, trans. G. Bull (Harmondsworth: Penguin, 1975), ch. VIII, p. 63). Because he wanted to convey the amoral connotations of Machiavelli's *virtù* and also 'avoid monotony', Bull translates it by the word 'prowess', at least in this chapter. See 'Introduction', pp. 24–5.

7   See, for example, ch. III of *The Prince*, pp. 34, 35, 42.

8   Ibid., ch. VII, p. 54.

9   N. Machiavelli, *Discourses on Livy*, trans. H. C. Mansfield and N. Tarcov (Chicago: University of Chicago Press, 1996), bk. II, preface, p. 123; bk. II, ch. 5, p. 140.

10   *The Prince*, ch. III, pp. 39–40.

11   J. G. A. Pocock, *The Machiavellian Moment: Florentine Political Thought and the Atlantic Republican Tradition* (Princeton: Princeton University Press, 1975), chs 3, 6–7; J. G. A. Pocock, 'Custom and grace, form and matter: an approach to Machiavelli's concept of innovation', in M. Fleisher (ed.), *Machiavelli and the Nature of Political Thought* (London: Croom Helm, 1973), pp. 153–74; Q. Skinner, 'Machiavelli's *Discorsi* and the pre-humanist origins of republican ideas', in G. Bock, Q. Skinner and M. Viroli (eds), *Machiavelli and Republicanism* (Cambridge: Cambridge University Press, 1990), pp. 121–41; and M. Viroli, *Machiavelli* (Oxford: Oxford University Press, 1998).

12   Pocock, *The Machiavellian Moment*, pp. 74–5.

13   Pocock, 'Custom and grace, form and matter', p. 173.

14   Skinner, 'Machiavelli's *Discorsi*', p. 141. To be fair, Skinner is careful to

set out the differences, as well as the similarities, between Machiavelli and earlier republican thinkers. Why he thinks that the 'positive resemblances' (p. 137) are more significant than the evident differences remains unexplained.

15   N. Machiavelli, *The History of Florence*, ed. H. Morley (London: Routledge and Sons, 1891), bk. VII, p. 326.

16   '. . . nature has created men so that they are able to desire everything and are unable to attain everything. So, since the desire is always greater than the power of acquiring, the result is discontent with what one possesses and a lack of satisfaction with it' (*Discourses*, bk. I, ch. 37, p. 78).

17   Ibid., bk. I, ch. 9, p. 29.

18   Ibid., bk. I, ch. 46; bk. III, ch. 8.

19   I. Berlin, 'The originality of Machiavelli', in *Against the Current: Essays in the History of Ideas* (London: Hogarth Press, 1979), p. 37.

20   *Discourses*, bk. I, ch. 2, pp. 11–13.

21   Berlin, 'The originality of Machiavelli', pp. 67–8.

22   E. Jacobitti, *Revolutionary Humanism and Historicism in Modern Italy* (New Haven and London: Yale University Press, 1981), p. 5.

23   'For since the inhabitants were sparse in the beginning of the world, they lived dispersed for a time like beasts; then, as generations multiplied, they gathered together, and to be able to defend themselves better, they began to look to whoever among them was more robust and of greater heart, and they made him a head, as it were, and obeyed him. From this arose the knowledge of things honest and good, differing from the pernicious and bad. For, seeing that if one individual hurt his benefactor, hatred and compassion among men came from it, and as they blamed the ungrateful and honoured those who were grateful, and thought too that those same injuries could be done to them, to escape like evil they were reduced to making laws and ordering punishments for whoever acted against them: hence came the knowledge of justice' (*Discourses*, bk. I, ch. 2, pp. 11–12).

24   F. Alderisio, *Machiavelli: l'arte dello stato nell'azione e negli scritti* (Bologna: Cesare Zuffi-Editore, 1950), p. 181.

25   Ibid., pp. 190, 186.

26   Ibid., pp. 195–6, 198, 200.

27   S. De Grazia, *Machiavelli in Hell* (Princeton: Princeton University Press, 1989), p. 31.

28   Ibid., pp. 119–20.

29   Ibid., pp. 69–70.

30   Ibid., p. 58.

31   Ibid., p. 89.

32   *Discourses*, bk. I, ch. 12, p. 36.

33   *The Prince*, ch. XI, p. 74.

34   *Discourses*, bk. I, ch. 11, p. 34.

[35] Ibid., bk. I, ch. 12, p. 37.

[36] Ibid., bk. I, ch. 12, p. 38.

[37] Ibid., bk. II, ch. 2, pp. 131–2.

[38] *The Prince*, ch. XII, p. 78.

[39] Ibid., ch. III, p. 35.

[40] Canto VII, *Inferno*, J. D. Sinclair (trans.), *The Divine Comedy of Dante Alighieri*, vol. 1 (New York: Oxford University Press, 1961), p. 103: 'He whose wisdom transcends all . . . ordained for worldly splendours a general minister and guide who should in due time change vain wealth from race to race and from one to another blood, beyond the prevention of human wits, so that one race rules and another languishes according to her sentence which is hidden like the snake in the grass. Your wisdom cannot strive with her. She foresees, judges and maintains her kingdom, as the other heavenly powers do theirs. Her changes have no respite. Necessity makes her swift, so fast men come to take their turn. This is she who is so reviled by the very men that should give her praise, laying on her wrongful blame and ill repute. But she is blest and does not hear it.'

[41] Machiavelli's actual phrasing betrays either his rapacious sex life or his lurid imagination: '. . . it is better to be impetuous than circumspect; because fortune is a woman and if she is to be submissive it is necessary to beat and coerce her. Experience shows that she is more often subdued by men who do this than by men who act coldly' (*The Prince*, ch. XXV, p. 133).

[42] Ibid., dedication to Lorenzo 'the Magnificent', p. 30.

[43] Ibid., ch. XXV, p. 130. See, also, *Discourses*, bk. II, ch. 30, pp. 199, 202.

[44] *Discourses*, bk. III, ch. 9, p. 240; *The Prince*, ch. XXV.

[45] *The Prince*, ch. XXV, p. 130.

[46] It is worth pointing out that Machiavelli wrote during a period of declining religious fervour and orthodoxy in Italy. His heterodoxy would not necessarily have stood out; nor, in the relatively tolerant climate of the time (before the Counter-Reformation), would it have exposed him to persecution. By the early sixteenth century, *naturalistic* humanism, associated with Pietro Pompanazzi and heavily influenced by the medieval Arab philosopher called Averroes, was challenging the pre-eminence of *religious* humanism. Pompanazzi taught that man's soul is mortal, indissolubly tied to the body, that supposedly supernatural events have natural explanations, and (like Averroes) that matter is eternal. It is significant that Machiavelli explicitly accepted the latter thesis, which apparently involves the denial of Creation (*Discourses*, bk. II, ch. 5). Many artists in the sixteenth century, while still producing religious work, no longer found creative inspiration in Christianity. With notable exceptions (such as Michelangelo), emotional profundity gave way to technical effect, the depiction of suffering and grief to harmonious patterns and literary symbolism. See E. Garin, *Dal Rinascimento all'Illuminismo* (Pisa: Nistri-Lischi Editori, 1970), p. 47; E. Cassirer,

P. O. Kristeller and J. H. Randall Jr. (eds), *The Renaissance Philosophy of Man: Selections in Translation* (Chicago: University of Chicago Press, 1948), editors' introduction, pp. 1–20; and V. Cronin, *The Flowering of the Renaissance* (London: Collins/Fontana, 1972), pp. 163–8.

47 F. De Sanctis, *Storia della letteratura italiana*, vol. 1, ed. B. Croce (Bari: Laterza, 1965), pp. 420–1.

4 The Empirical Method

1 J. Burnham, *The Machiavellians: Defenders of Freedom* (Washington, DC: Gateway, 1943), p. 84.

2 C. S. Singleton, 'The perspective of art', *The Kenyon Review*, XV (1953), 180–9.

3 E. Cassirer, *The Myth of the State* (New Haven, Conn.: Yale University Press, 1946), pp. 153–6.

4 L. Olschki, *Machiavelli the Scientist* (Berkeley: The Gillick Press, 1945), pp. 22–33. It is unclear what Olschki means when he claims that, for Galileo, 'matter is unalterable', since the great astronomer evidently thought that matter undergoes incessant change. Perhaps what is meant is that Galileo, like Copernicus, reduced all nature to one system, homogeneous in substance, and subject to the same laws. That is to say, matter is constant in the sense that it always conforms to the same mathematically formulable principles. For another classic interpretation of Machiavelli as a scientist, see L. Russo, *Machiavelli* (Bari: Laterza, 1949), especially p. 214, where the author writes: 'Liberty or authority, republic or principate, are the *subject* but not, in the Kantian sense, the *form* of Machiavelli's thinking' – the 'form' being scientific.

5 M. Viroli, *Machiavelli* (Oxford: Oxford University Press, 1998), pp. 1–3, 64, 70.

6 N. Machiavelli, *The Prince*, trans. G. Bull (Harmondsworth: Penguin, 1975), ch. III, p. 44.

7 N. Machiavelli, *Discourses on Livy*, trans. H. C. Mansfield and N. Tarcov (Chicago: University of Chicago Press, 1996), bk. III, ch. 43, p. 302.

8 *The Prince*, ch. III, p. 35.

9 Viroli, *Machiavelli*, p. 3.

10 M. A. Finocchiaro, *Galileo on the World Systems: A New Abridged Translation and Guide* (Berkeley: University of California Press, 1997), pp. 6–7, 356–72.

11 B. Fontana, *Hegemony and Power: On the Relation between Gramsci and Machiavelli* (Minneapolis: University of Minnesota Press, 1993), pp. 79–80.

12 *The Prince*, ch. XV, pp. 90–1.

13 *Discourses*, bk. I, preface, p. 5.

[14]   Ibid., bk. I, preface, p. 6.
[15]   H. Butterfield, *The Statecraft of Machiavelli* (London: G. Bell & Sons, 1940), p. 57.
[16]   F. Gilbert, *Machiavelli and Guicciardini* (Princeton: Princeton University Press, 1965), p. 170.
[17]   See S. Anglo, *Machiavelli: A Dissection* (London: Paladin, 1971), ch. 9.
[18]   F. Chabod, *Machiavelli and the Renaissance*, trans. D. Moore (New York: Harper & Row, 1958), p. 113.
[19]   *Discourses*, bk. III, ch. 43, p. 302.
[20]   Ibid., bk. I, ch. 37, pp. 78, 80; bk. I, ch. 39, pp. 83–4.
[21]   Ibid., bk. I, ch. 11, p. 36 (translation amended by J.F.)
[22]   E. Garin, *Dal Rinascimento all'Illuminismo* (Pisa: Nistri-Lischi Editori, 1970), p. 49.
[23]   Butterfield, *The Statecraft of Machiavelli*, pp. 30–1.
[24]   F. Guicciardini, *Maxims and Reflections of a Renaissance Statesman*, trans. M. Domandi (New York: Harper & Row, 1965), C, 110.
[25]   Ibid., B, 61; F. Guicciardini, 'Considerations on the "Discourses" of Machiavelli', in *Selected Writings*, trans. C. and M. Grayson (London: Oxford University Press, 1965), pp. 110–12.
[26]   A. J. Parel, *The Machiavellian Cosmos* (New Haven and London: Yale University Press, 1992), especially the 'Introduction' and 'Conclusion'.
[27]   Burnham, *The Machiavellians*, p. 38.
[28]   J. Kraft, 'Truth and poetry in Machiavelli', *Journal of Modern History*, XXIII (1951), 109–10.
[29]   Butterfield, *The Statecraft of Machiavelli*, p. 126.
[30]   J. Plamenatz, *Man and Society*, vol. 1 (London: Longmans, 1968), pp. 3–4.
[31]   T. Kuhn, *The Copernican Revolution* (Cambridge, Mass.: Harvard University Press, 1957), p. 92.
[32]   *Discourses*, bk. I, ch. 56.
[33]   Ibid., bk. I, ch. 56, p. 114. Eugenio Garin thinks that Machiavelli is being 'ironic' here (*Dal Rinascimento all'Illuminismo*, p. 59).
[34]   *The Prince*, ch. XVIII, p. 100.
[35]   In a passage from *The Art of War* quoted by Parel, *The Machiavellian Cosmos*, p. 62. Oddly, Parel cites this passage in support of his thesis that Machiavelli was a superstitious pagan, when in fact it suggests that he was neither superstitious nor a pagan.
[36]   S. Greer, *The Logic of Social Inquiry* (Chicago: Aldine Publishing Co., 1969), p. 178.
[37]   *Discourses*, bk. I, chs 26, 30; bk. II, ch. 23.
[38]   Ibid., bk. II, preface, p. 123.
[39]   Ibid., bk. II, preface, p. 125.
[40]   Kraft, 'Truth and poetry in Machiavelli', 117– 18.
[41]   V. Pareto, *The Mind and Society*, trans. A. Bongiorno and A. Livingstone

(London: Jonathan Cape, 1935), para. 2532; G. Mosca, *The Ruling Class*, trans. H. D. Kahn (New York: McGraw Hill, 1939), p. 43.

[42] J. R. Hale, *Machiavelli and Renaissance Italy* (London: English Universities Press, 1961), pp. 151–5.

[43] See, for example, Butterfield, *The Statecraft of Machiavelli*, p. 71.

[44] *The Prince*, ch. IX, p. 69.

[45] Ibid., ch. XX, p. 114.

[46] *Discourses*, bk. I, ch. 18, p. 49.

[47] *The Prince*, ch. IV, pp. 45–6. See ch. XXV as well.

[48] *Discourses*, bk. III, ch. 9, p. 240. In *The Prince*, Machiavelli declares: 'I also believe that the one who adapts his policy to the times prospers, and likewise that the one whose policy clashes with the demands of the times does not' (ch. XXV, p. 131).

[49] *Discourses*, bk. III, ch. 21, pp. 262–3.

[50] *The Prince*, ch. XII, pp. 77–80. For another example of Machiavelli's readiness to consider inconvenient evidence, see ibid., ch. XIX, pp. 106–14.

[51] J. Hankins, 'Humanism and the origins of modern political thought', in J. Kraye (ed.), *The Cambridge Companion to Renaissance Humanism* (Cambridge: Cambridge University Press, 1996), p. 121.

[52] Burnham, *The Machiavellians*, pp. 55–6.

[53] *The Prince*, ch. III.

[54] Ibid., ch. III, p. 40.

[55] Ibid., ch. III, pp. 39–40; *Discourses*, bk. III, ch. 1, p. 209.

[56] H. Baron, 'Towards a more positive evaluation of the fifteenth-century Renaissance', *Journal of the History of Ideas*, IV (1943), 37, 46.

[57] Pareto, *The Mind and Society*, para. 69.

5   Political Realism

[1] N. Machiavelli, *The Prince*, trans. G. Bull (Harmondsworth: Penguin, 1975), ch. XV, pp. 90–1.

[2] Ibid., ch. XVII, p. 96.

[3] N. Machiavelli, *Discourses on Livy*, trans. H. C. Mansfield and N. Tarcov (Chicago: University of Chicago Press, 1996), bk. I, ch. 3, p. 15.

[4] Ibid., bk. I, ch. 37, p. 78.

[5] Ibid., bk. II, ch. 19, p. 173.

[6] Ibid., bk. I, ch. 37, p. 78.

[7] *The Prince*, chs III–V. See, also, *Discourses*, bk. III, ch. 5, p. 217, where Machiavelli writes: 'Thus princes may know that they begin to lose their state at the hour they begin to break the laws and those modes and those customs that are ancient, under which men have lived a long time.'

[8] *The Prince*, ch. XVIII.

[9]   Ibid., ch. XIX, p. 113.

[10] Ibid., ch. XVIII, pp. 100–1. Anyone who thinks that this view of mass gulli-
      bility is confined to *The Prince* should consult bk. I, ch. 25, p. 60 of the
      Discourses, where Machiavelli declares: 'For the generality of men feed on
      what appears as much as on what is; indeed, many times they are moved
      more by things that appear than by things that are.' Elsewhere in the
      Discourses (bk. I, ch. 53, p. 106), Machiavelli claims that the people, when
      consulted, tend to endorse superficially attractive policies and reject super-
      ficially unattractive policies, oblivious to the losses or gains 'concealed
      underneath'.

[11] *Discourses*, bk. II, chs. 4, 13, 19.

[12] Ibid., bk. II, ch. 17, p. 165.

[13] Ibid., bk. I, ch. 3, p. 15.

[14] *The Prince*, ch. XVII, p. 96.

[15] 'Because one cannot give a certain remedy for such disorders that arise in
      republics, it follows that it is impossible to order a perpetual republic,
      because its ruin is caused through a thousand unexpected ways'
      (*Discourses*, bk. III, ch. 17, p. 257).

[16] Ibid., bk. II, preface, p. 123.

[17] N. Machiavelli, *The History of Florence*, ed. H. Morley (London: Routledge
      and Sons, 1891), bk. V, p. 227.

[18] *Discourses*, bk. II, ch. 25, p. 190.

[19] Ibid., bk. I, ch. 9, p. 29.

[20] Ibid., bk. I, ch. 16, p. 46.

[21] Ibid., bk. I, ch. 44, p. 92.

[22] Ibid., bk. II, chs. 17, 35, 55; bk. III, ch. 8; *The Prince*, ch. VI.

[23] *Discourses*, bk. I, chs. 1, 11; *The Prince*, ch. VII.

[24] M. Viroli, 'Machiavelli and the republican idea of politics', in G. Bock,
      Q. Skinner and M. Viroli (eds), *Machiavelli and Republicanism*
      (Cambridge: Cambridge University Press, 1990), p. 146.

[25] B. Fontana, *Hegemony and Power: On the Relation between Gramsci and
      Machiavelli* (Minneapolis: University of Minnesota Press, 1993), pp. 123,
      125–6.

[26] Ibid., pp. 149, 161.

[27] F. E. Adcock, *Roman Political Ideas and Practice* (Ann Arbor: University of
      Michigan Press, 1964), pp. 14, 46.

[28] *Discourses*, bk. I, ch. 6, p. 21; *The Prince*, ch. XXI, p. 123.

[29] *Discourses*, bk. I, ch. 20.

[30] Ibid., bk. I, chs. 29, 30.

[31] Ibid., bk. I, ch. 58, p. 117.

[32] Ibid., bk. I, ch. 54.

[33] Ibid., bk. II, ch. 2, pp. 130–3; bk. III, ch. 9, p. 240.

[34] Ibid., bk. II, ch. 2, p. 129; bk. II, ch. 19, pp. 172–3. Machiavelli's depiction

of republics as naturally aggrandizing was novel, though it was prefigured, a century earlier, in the writings of civic humanists such as Leonardo Bruni who praised heroic actions and celebrated *gloria* and *grandezza* (grandeur, magnitude) as the highest goals to which a city could aspire. See L. Bruni, *Laudatio Florentinae Urbis* (1403–4), in H. Baron, *From Petrarch to Leonardo Bruni* (Chicago: University of Chicago Press, 1968), pp. 217–63.

35 N. Wood, 'The value of asocial sociability: contributions of Machiavelli, Sidney and Montesquieu', in M. Fleisher (ed.), *Machiavelli and the Nature of Political Thought* (London: Croom Helm, 1973), pp. 282–91 in particular.

36 *Discourses*, bk. I, ch. 4, p. 16.

37 Ibid., bk. I, chs. 3–5.

38 *History of Florence*, bk. VII, pp. 326–7. For an illuminating discussion of Machiavelli's views on social conflict, see G. Bock, 'Civil discord in Machiavelli's *Istorie Fiorentine*', in Bock et al. (eds), *Machiavelli and Republicanism*, pp. 181–201.

39 *Discourses*, bk. I, ch. 2.

40 Given this clear Machiavellian injunction, effectively repeated over and over again in passage after passage of realist analysis, it is odd that Fontana should portray the Florentine as a utopian who 'teaches citizens to love one another' and envisages a world where 'domination/subordination structures' are abolished, 'where social and political life is grounded on the reciprocity and mutuality of equal speech and discourse' (*Hegemony and Power*, pp. 114, 162). No one can doubt the originality of this interpretation, but surely Fontana is the gentlest of Conor Cruise O'Brien's 'gentle Machiavellians', who feel compelled, by admiration for the great man, to exaggerate his democratic and libertarian tendencies, and to expurgate all those passages where he defends cruelty and deception as tools of governance. As O'Brien writes, 'the trouble with liking him [Machiavelli] is that it can prevent one from hearing what he is actually saying' (*The Suspecting Glance* (London: Faber and Faber, 1972), pp. 16–17).

41 *Discourses*, bk. I, ch. 34, pp. 74–5.

42 T. Aquinas, *Summa Theologiae*, vol. 28, ed. T. Gilby (London: Blackfriars, 1966), pp. 43, 127.

43 F. Chabod, *Machiavelli and the Renaissance*, trans. D. Moore (New York: Harper & Row, 1958), pp. 164–5.

44 F. Guicciardini, 'Considerations on the "Discourses" of Machiavelli', in *Selected Writings*, trans. C. and M. Grayson (London: Oxford University Press, 1965), p. 92.

45 *Discourses*, bk. III, ch. 27, pp. 274–5.

46 Ibid., bk. III, ch. 41, p. 301.

47 B. Croce, *Elementi di politica* (Bari: Laterza, 1925), pp. 59–66.

48 Berlin notwithstanding, the substance of Croce's thesis is still taken for granted by many – especially by philosophers who reflect on the issue of

'dirty hands'. For example, Michael Walzer says of Machiavelli: 'His political judgments are indeed consequentialist in character, but not his moral
judgments. We know whether cruelty is used well or badly by its effects
over time. But that it is bad to use cruelty we know in some other way. The
deceitful and cruel politician is excused (if he succeeds) only in the sense
that the rest of us come to agree that the results were "worth it" or, more
likely, that we simply forget his crimes when we praise his success'
(M. Walzer, 'Political action: the problem of dirty hands', *Philosophy and
Public Affairs*, 2 (Winter 1973), 175). Similarly, Steven Lukes writes that,
for Machiavelli, 'deception, betrayal, and worse, when they are committed
for the public good, violate morally important principles and commit
uncancelled wrongs' (S. Lukes, 'Marxism and dirty hands', in *Moral
Conflict and Politics* (Oxford: Clarendon Press, 1991), p. 197). Croce's picture of Machiavelli as a tortured soul also remains fairly common in the
secondary literature. Eugenio Garin is being representative when he refers
to the Florentine's 'tragic sense of life's conflicts', and 'sorrowful consciousness of the dramatic shifts in human fortune' (*Dal Rinascimento
all'Illuminismo* (Pisa: Nistri-Lischi Editori, 1970), p. 46).

49   I. Berlin, 'The originality of Machiavelli', in *Against the Current: Essays in
the History of Ideas* (London: Hogarth Press, 1979), p. 45.

50   Ibid., pp. 46–50.

51   J. Hankins, 'Humanism and the origins of modern political thought', in
J. Kraye (ed.), *The Cambridge Companion to Renaissance Humanism*
(Cambridge and New York: Cambridge University Press, 1996), p. 136;
M. Hulliung, *Citizen Machiavelli* (Princeton: Princeton University Press,
1983), p. 8.

52   A. W. H. Adkins, *Moral Values and Political Behaviour in Ancient Greece*
(London: Chatto & Windus, 1972).

53   A. MacIntyre, *A Short History of Ethics* (London: Routledge & Kegan
Paul, 1967), pp. 5–7, 90.

54   P. Burke, *The Italian Renaissance: Culture and Society in Italy*
(Cambridge: Polity Press, 1986), pp. 198–200.

55   B. P. Copenhaver and C. B. Schmitt, *Renaissance Philosophy* (Oxford and
New York: Oxford University Press, 1992), pp. 211–12. But if Anthony
Quinton is right, 'Christian hedonism' is an oxymoron, since Christianity's
'conception of the happiness or well-being of mankind was ascetical and
non-hedonistic'. As humankind's 'greatest felicity', the 'beatific vision of
God', is to be enjoyed after bodily death, it is detached from 'the natural
earthly satisfactions'. Indeed, a preoccupation with such satisfactions may
impede our path to salvation and – hence – true felicity (A. Quinton,
Utilitarian Ethics (London: Duckworth, 1973), p. 12).

56   E. Cassirer, *The Myth of the State* (New Haven, Conn.: Yale University
Press, 1946), p. 154.

57 *Discourses*, bk. I, ch. 26, pp. 61–2.

58 *The Prince*, ch. XV, p. 91; ch. XVIII, p. 99.

59 Ibid., ch. XVII, p. 95.

60 Ibid., ch. XVIII, pp. 101–2.

61 *Discourses*, bk. I, ch. 9, p. 29.

62 Walzer, 'Political action: the problem of dirty hands', p. 175.

63 *Discourses*, bk. II, preface, p. 125.

64 Ibid., bk. I, ch. 2, p. 10; bk. I, ch. 11, p. 35; bk. I, ch. 17, p. 48; bk. II, ch. 18, p. 171.

65 *The Prince*, ch. XVIII, p. 101.

66 Ibid., ch. XVIII, pp. 100–1.

67 *Discourses*, bk. II, ch. 2, pp. 131–2; bk. III, ch. 1, pp. 211–12.

68 M. Viroli, *Machiavelli* (Oxford: Oxford University Press, 1998), pp. 121, 123.

69 Ibid., p. 135.

70 *Discourses*, bk. I, ch. 7, pp. 23–4.

71 Ibid., bk. III, ch. 41, p. 301.

72 Ibid., bk. I, ch. 18, pp. 50–1.

73 Ibid., bk. I, ch. 15, p. 43; bk. I, ch. 23, p. 57; bk. I, ch. 31, pp. 69–70; bk. II, ch. 21; bk. II, ch. 24, p. 188; bk. III, ch. 17; bk. III, ch. 41, pp. 300–1.

74 Ibid., bk. I, ch. 2, pp. 13–14; bk. I, ch. 4; bk. I, ch. 5, pp. 17–18; bk. I, ch. 13, p. 40; bk. I, ch. 16, pp. 44–6; bk. I, ch. 17, p. 48; bk. I, ch. 28; bk. I, ch. 35; bk. I, ch. 37, p. 80; bk. I, ch. 40, p. 87; bk. I, ch. 47, p. 98; bk. I, ch. 49, p. 100; bk. II, ch. 2, pp. 129–32; bk. III, ch. 5, p. 217; bk. III, ch. 7; bk. III, ch. 8, p. 239; bk. III, ch. 25, p. 271; bk. III, ch. 28, p. 276. See, also, *The Prince*, ch. V.

75 *Discourses*, bk. I, ch. 1, p. 7. For an interesting analysis of Machiavelli's concept of freedom, see Q. Skinner, 'The paradoxes of political liberty', in S. M. McMurrin (ed.), *The Tanner Lectures on Human Values*, vol. VII (Cambridge and London: Cambridge University Press, 1986), pp. 225–50. In this and similar papers, Skinner argues that Machiavelli articulated a distinctively republican, as opposed to liberal, theory of political freedom, since he saw freedom and legal constraint as mutually supportive. Although, according to Skinner, he held a 'negative' idea of liberty as the non-obstruction of individual agents in pursuit of their own goals, he understood that liberty requires a healthy social and political context: apathy and chaos bring tyranny and servitude. Only if we discharge the full range of our civic duties and behave with public spirit can society hold together and prosper. But such virtuous activity does not come naturally; it is a product of good laws that alter our habitual patterns of selfish behaviour. Skinner gives the example of constitutional checks and balances, which ensure that self-interested groups will need to compromise in order to achieve their public policy objectives. The law, on this understanding,

preserves our liberty not merely by coercing others who might prevent us from acting as we choose, but also by coercing, or perhaps encouraging, each one of us to act in a particular way. Skinner is right to say that Machiavelli's concept of liberty is essentially negative, as it does not connect liberty to the metaphysical idea of self-realization. He is also correct in his conclusion that Machiavelli was not a 'rights' theorist who saw the law as nothing but a means of protecting individual security or autonomy. But I cannot share Skinner's implicit assumption that Machiavelli's view of law as the general condition of personal liberty falls outside the parameters of liberal discourse. The legal enforcement of civic duties has always been accepted by liberals – especially those of the utilitarian persuasion – in both theory and practice. J. S. Mill, to take one prominent example, made it plain that we could legitimately be coerced into jury duty, military service, payment of taxes and other, less obvious civic responsibilities. Ever since Tocqueville, liberals have recognized that apathy and rampant individualism could spell the death of liberty, and that civic-minded behaviour was the lifeblood of a free society. As for the use of constitutional mechanisms to channel selfish intentions into socially constructive outcomes, this is a central axiom of liberalism in all its forms. Another oddity of Skinner's argument is brilliantly explored by Paul A. Rahe. Machiavelli, Skinner acknowledges, jettisoned the linkage between freedom and natural teleology. But, since *classical* republicanism presupposes an Aristotelian doctrine of *eudaimonia* or human flourishing, his persistence in describing Machiavelli as a *classical* republican is a source of puzzlement. Rahe thinks that Skinner, because of his well-known methodological commitments, cannot entertain the possibility that Machiavelli was a radical innovator. As a consequence, he has to be situated within a recognizable and established linguistic context ('Situating Machiavelli', in J. Hankins (ed.), *Renaissance Civic Humanism* (Cambridge: Cambridge University Press, 2000), pp. 270–308).

76 *Discourses*, bk. I, ch. 16, p. 45–6.
77 Ibid., bk. III, ch. 25, p. 271.
78 Ibid., bk. II, ch. 2, p. 132.
79 For a useful, albeit brief, analysis of the distinction between rule and act utilitarianism, see W. Kymlicka, *Contemporary Political Philosophy: An Introduction* (Oxford: Clarendon Press, 1990), pp. 27–9.

6   The Legacy

1 K. Minogue, 'Method in intellectual history: Quentin Skinner's *Foundations*', in J. Tully (ed.), *Meaning and Context: Quentin Skinner and his Critics* (Cambridge: Polity Press, 1988), pp. 185–6.

2 J. G. A. Pocock, *The Machiavellian Moment: Florentine Political Thought and the Atlantic Republican Tradition* (Princeton: Princeton University Press, 1975).

3 N. Machiavelli, *Discourses on Livy*, trans. H. C. Mansfield and N. Tarcov (Chicago: University of Chicago Press, 1996), bk. I, ch. 6, p. 23.

4 F. Guicciardini, 'Considerations on the "Discourses" of Machiavelli', in *Selected Writings*, trans. C. and M. Grayson (London: Oxford University Press, 1965), p. 89.

5 N. Machiavelli, *The Prince*, trans. G. Bull (Harmondsworth: Penguin, 1975), ch. V, pp. 48–9.

6 *Discourses*, bk. I, ch. 26, p. 61.

7 *The Prince*, ch. III, p. 36.

8 Ibid., ch. XIX, p. 102.

9 For example, Machiavelli praised the Roman general Fabius Maximus, who 'saved the state for the Romans' by *deferring combat* with Hannibal: 'Everyone knows that Fabius Maximus proceeded hesitantly and cautiously with his army, far from all impetuosity and from all Roman audacity, and good fortune made this mode of his match well with the times. For when Hannibal, young and with fresh fortune, had come into Italy and had already defeated the Roman people two times, and when that republic was almost deprived of its good military and was terrified, better fortune could not have come than to have a captain who held the enemy at bay with his slowness and caution' (*Discourses*, bk. III, ch. 10, p. 242; bk. III, ch. 9, p. 239).

10 *The Prince*, ch. XV, pp. 90–1.

11 *Discourses*, bk. I, ch. 3, p. 15; bk. I, ch. 6, p. 21.

12 A. Gramsci, *Quaderni del carcere*, vol. III, ed. V. Gerratana (Turin: Einaudi, 1975), p. 1601.

13 *The Prince*, ch. XV, p. 91.

14 C. S. Singleton, 'The perspective of art', *The Kenyon Review*, XV (1953), 182, 185–6.

15 S. S. Wolin, *Politics and Vision: Continuity and Innovation in Western Political Thought* (London: Allen & Unwin Ltd., 1961), p. 237.

16 Ibid., p. 232.

17 *Discourses*, bk. I, ch. 5, p. 19.

18 Ibid., bk. I, ch. 4.

19 B. Croce, *Elementi di politica* (Bari: Laterza, 1925), pp. 59–67; F. Chabod, *Machiavelli and the Renaissance*, trans. D. Moore (New York: Harper & Row, 1958), p. 142.

20 B. P. Copenhaver and C. B. Schmitt, *Renaissance Philosophy* (Oxford and New York: Oxford University Press, 1992), p. 151.

21 Croce, *Elementi di politica*, pp. 66–7.

22 *Discourses*, bk. III, ch. 3, p. 215.

[23] Ibid., bk. III, ch. 11, p. 244.

[24] M. Hulliung, *Citizen Machiavelli* (Princeton: Princeton University Press, 1983), pp. 222–3.

[25] C. L. Becker, *The Heavenly City of the Eighteenth-Century Philosophers* (New Haven and London: Yale University Press, 1932).

[26] Ibid., p. 6.

[27] Ibid., p. 43.

[28] A.-N. de Condorcet, *Sketch for a Historical Picture of the Progress of the Human Mind* (Westport, Conn.: Hyperion Press Inc., 1979), pp. 4, 200.

[29] Becker, *The Heavenly City*, p. 19.

[30] Ibid., p. 15.

[31] T. Hobbes, *Leviathan*, ed. J. Plamenatz (London: The Fontana Library, 1962), p. 82.

[32] Ibid., 'Introduction' by J. Plamenatz, pp. 17–18.

[33] Ibid., p. 145.

[34] Ibid., p. 90.

[35] D. Hume, *A Treatise of Human Nature*, bk. I, ed. D. G. C. Macnabb (London: The Fontana Library, 1962), p. 42.

[36] Ibid.

[37] J. Bentham, *Anarchical Fallacies*, in J. Waldron (ed.), *Nonsense upon Stilts: Bentham, Burke and Marx on the Rights of Man* (London and New York: Methuen, 1987), p. 53.

[38] Ibid., pp. 48, 74.

[39] Pocock, *The Machiavellian Moment*, pp. 462, 506, 545–52. Pocock does not actually provide much direct evidence for his characterization of American colonial culture. He relies heavily on controversial studies by other historians, particularly Gordon S. Wood's *The Creation of the American Republic* (Chapel Hill: University of North Carolina Press, 1969). For Wood, the Revolution was not about the preservation of colonial tax-exemptions but rather about brotherhood, self-sacrifice and community – all classical republican virtues. His thesis has been challenged by a number of scholars; see, for example, P. A. Rahe, *Republics Ancient and Modern: Classical Republicanism and the American Tradition* (Chapel Hill: University of North Carolina Press, 1992).

[40] J. Madison, 'Federalist no. 10', in A. Hamilton, J. Madison and J. Jay, *Selections from The Federalist*, ed. H. S. Commager (New York: Appleton-Century-Crofts, Inc., 1949), pp. 11–12. First published in 1787.

[41] Ibid., pp. 10–11.

[42] E. Jacobitti, *Revolutionary Humanism and Historicism in Modern Italy* (New Haven and London: Yale University Press, 1981), p. 6.

[43] Ibid., p. 52.

[44] V. Pareto, *The Mind and Society*, trans. A. Bongiorno and A. Livingston (London: Jonathan Cape, 1935), para. 6.

45 Ibid., paras 11, 19.
46 Ibid., paras 69, 506.
47 G. Mosca, *The Ruling Class*, trans. H. D. Kahn (New York: McGraw Hill, 1939), p. 125.
48 Ibid., p. 176.
49 Ibid., p. 128.
50 Pareto, *The Mind and Society*, para. 2410.
51 Ibid., para. 1975.
52 See, for example, ibid., paras 1158, 1704, 2166, 2262, 2535.
53 G. Mosca, 'Il "Principe" di Machiavelli quattro secoli dopo la morte del suo autore', in *Ciò che la storia potrebbe insegnare* (Milan: Giuffrè, 1958), pp. 708, 719. First published in 1927.
54 Mosca, *The Ruling Class*, pp. 202–3.
55 Ibid., pp. 193, 450.
56 Pareto, *The Mind and Society*, para. 2459.
57 Mosca, *The Ruling Class*, p. 71.
58 Ibid., p. 39.
59 Pareto, *The Mind and Society*, para. 2178.
60 Mosca, *The Ruling Class*, p. 457.
61 Ibid., p. 288.
62 Ibid., p. 292.
63 Ibid., p. 196; and G. Mosca, *Partiti e sindacati nella crisi del regime parlamentare* (Bari: Laterza, 1949), p. 35.
64 T. Sowell, *A Conflict of Visions* (New York: William Morrow, 1987), ch. 2.
65 K. Marx, 'Economic and philosophic manuscripts' (1844), in L. D. Easton and K. H. Guddat (trans. and eds), *Writings of the Young Marx on Philosophy and Society* (New York: Doubleday, 1967), p. 304.
66 B. Croce, *Materialismo storico ed economia marxista* (Bari: Laterza, 1927), p. 112. First published in 1899.
67 Ibid., pp. xii–xiv. From the preface to the 1917 edition.
68 Gramsci, *Quaderni del carcere*, vol. III, p. 1710. See, also, p. 1564, where Gramsci praises Machiavelli for understanding that the choice between a dictatorship and a republic could not be based on principle, since this would involve the (un-Marxist) hypostatization of the concept of liberty.
69 Ibid., vol. II, p. 764.
70 Ibid., vol. II, pp. 1334, 1402.
71 Ibid., vol. II, p. 1437.
72 Ibid., vol. III, p. 1599.
73 Ibid., vol. III, p. 1572.
74 Ibid., vol. III, p. 1578.
75 S. Pinker, *The Blank Slate: The Modern Denial of Human Nature* (London: Penguin, 2002), part I.
76 Ibid., p. 6.

[77] Ibid., part I, ch. 3, provides a masterly summary of these developments.

[78] Ibid., part I.

[79] Ibid., p. 56. In support of what he says in this passage, Pinker cites the following studies: D. Freeman, *The Fateful Hoaxing of Margaret Mead: a Historical Analysis of her Samoan Research* (Boulder, Col.: Westview Press, 1999); and R. W. Wrangham and D. Peterson, *Demonic Males: Apes and the Origins of Human Violence* (Boston: Houghton Mifflin, 1996).

[80] L. Keeley, *War before Civilization: the Myth of the Peaceful Savage* (New York: Oxford University Press, 1996), p. 90.

[81] *Discourses*, bk. I, ch. 6.

[82] 'This is the way things are: whenever one tries to escape one danger one runs into another. Prudence consists in being able to assess the nature of a particular threat and in accepting the lesser evil' (*The Prince*, ch. XXI, p. 123).

[83] Ibid., ch. XVIII, pp. 100–1.

[84] For some useful analyses of 'trust' and its role in social interaction, see M. E. Warren (ed.), *Democracy and Trust* (Cambridge: Cambridge University Press, 1999).

[85] For a penetrating discussion of the different theories of international relations, see D. Boucher, *Political Theories of International Relations* (Oxford: Oxford University Press, 1998).

[86] A view developed by Hedley Bull in *The Anarchical Society: A Study of Order in World Politics* (London: Macmillan, 1984).

[87] C. Cruise O'Brien, *The Suspecting Glance* (London: Faber and Faber, 1972), p. 16.

[88] L. Strauss, *Thoughts on Machiavelli* (Chicago and London: University of Chicago Press, 1958), p. 295.

[89] Hulliung, *Citizen Machiavelli*, pp. 223, 251.

[90] N. Bobbio, *Saggi sulla scienza politica in Italia* (Bari: Laterza, 1977), pp. 9–10.

[91] D. Zolo, *Democracy and Complexity* (Cambridge: Polity Press, 1992), p. 6.

[92] Wolin, *Politics and Vision*, p. 216.

Select Bibliography

Works by Niccolò Machiavelli

Machiavelli: The Chief Works and Others, ed. and trans. A. Gilbert (Durham, NC: Duke University Press, 1989), 3 vols.

The Art of War [1521], in *Chief Works*, pp. 561–726.

Discourses on Livy [1531], trans. H. C. Mansfield and N. Tarcov (Chicago: University of Chicago Press, 1996).

The History of Florence [1527], ed. H. Morley (London: Routledge and Sons, 1891).

The Legations, in *Chief Works*, pp. 120–60.

The Literary Works of Machiavelli, ed. and trans. J. R. Hale (Oxford: Oxford University Press, 1961).

Opere Complete, ed. S. Bertelli and F. Gaeta (Milan: Feltrinelli, 1960–5), 8 vols.

The Prince [1531], trans. G. Bull (Harmondsworth: Penguin, 1975).

Other Sources

Adcock, F. E., *Roman Political Ideas and Practice* (Ann Arbor: University of Michigan Press, 1964).

Adkins, A. W. H., *Moral Values and Political Behaviour in Ancient Greece* (London: Chatto & Windus, 1972).

Alderisio, F., *Machiavelli: l'arte dello stato nell'azione e negli scritti* (Bologna: Cesare Zuffi-Editore, 1950).

Anglo, S., *Machiavelli: A Dissection* (London: Paladin, 1971).

Aquinas, T., *Summa Theologiae*, vol. 28, ed. T. Gilby (London: Blackfriars, 1966).

Avery, C., *Florentine Renaissance Sculpture* (London: John Murray, 1970).

Baron, H., 'Machiavelli: the republican citizen and the author of "The Prince" ', *English Historical Review*, 76 (1961).

——, 'Towards a more positive evaluation of the fifteenth-century Renaissance', *Journal of the History of Ideas*, IV (1943).

Becker, C. L., *The Heavenly City of the Eighteenth-Century Philosophers* (New Haven and London: Yale University Press, 1932).

Bentham, J., *Anarchical Fallacies*, in J. Waldron (ed.), *Nonsense upon Stilts: Bentham, Burke and Marx on the Rights of Man* (London and New York: Methuen, 1987).

Berlin, I., 'The originality of Machiavelli', in *Against the Current: Essays in the History of Ideas* (London: Hogarth Press, 1979).

Black, R., 'Machiavelli, servant of the Florentine Republic', in G. Bock, Q. Skinner and M. Viroli (eds), *Machiavelli and Republicanism* (Cambridge: Cambridge University Press, 1990).

Bobbio, N., *Saggi sulla scienza politica in Italia* (Bari: Laterza, 1977).

Bock, G., 'Civil discord in Machiavelli's *Istorie Fiorentine*', in G. Bock, Q. Skinner and M. Viroli (eds), *Machiavelli and Republicanism* (Cambridge: Cambridge University Press, 1990).

Boucher, D., *Political Theories of International Relations* (Oxford: Oxford University Press, 1998).

——, 'The duplicitous Machiavelli', *Machiavelli Studies*, 3 (1990).

Brucker, G. A., *Renaissance Florence* (New York: John Wiley & Sons, 1969).

Bruni, L., *Laudatio Florentinae Urbis*, in H. Baron, *From Petrarch to Leonardo Bruni* (Chicago: University of Chicago Press, 1968). Composed in 1403–4.

Bull, H., *The Anarchical Society: A Study of Order in World Politics* (London: Macmillan, 1984).

Burckhardt, J., *The Civilization of the Renaissance in Italy*, trans. S. G. C. Middlemore (New York: Harper & Row, 1958), 2 vols. First published in 1860.

Burke, P., *The Italian Renaissance: Culture and Society in Italy* (Cambridge: Polity Press, 1986).

Burnham, J., *The Machiavellians: Defenders of Freedom* (Washington DC: Gateway, 1943).

Butterfield, H., *The Statecraft of Machiavelli* (London: G. Bell & Sons, 1940).

Cassirer, E., *The Myth of the State* (New Haven, Conn.: Yale University Press, 1946).

——, Kristeller, P. O., and Randall, J. H. Jr. (eds), 'Introduction' to *The Renaissance Philosophy of Man: Selections in Translation* (Chicago: University of Chicago Press, 1948).

Chabod, F., *Machiavelli and the Renaissance*, trans. D. Moore (New York: Harper & Row, 1958).

Cochrane, E., 'Machiavelli: 1940–60', *Journal of Modern History*, 33 (1961).

Condorcet, A.-N. de, *Sketch for a Historical Picture of the Progress of the Human Mind* (Westport, Conn.: Hyperion Press Inc., 1979).

Copenhaver, B. P., and Schmitt, C. B., *Renaissance Philosophy* (Oxford and New York: Oxford University Press, 1992).

Croce, B., *Elementi di politica* (Bari: Laterza, 1925).

——, *Materialismo storico ed economia marxista* (Bari: Laterza, 1927).

Cronin, V., *The Flowering of the Renaissance* (London: Collins/Fontana, 1972).

Danby, J. F., *Shakespeare's Doctrine of Nature: a Study of King Lear* (London: Faber, 1961).

Dante Alighieri, *The Divine Comedy*, trans. J. D. Sinclair (New York: Oxford University Press, 1961), vol. 1 (*Inferno*).

De Grazia, S., *Machiavelli in Hell* (Princeton: Princeton University Press, 1989).

De Sanctis, F., *Storia della letteratura italiana*, vol. 1, ed. B. Croce (Bari: Laterza, 1965).

Femia, J. V., *The Machiavellian Legacy: Essays in Italian Political Thought* (Basingstoke: Macmillan, 1998).

——, 'Machiavelli', in D. Boucher and P. Kelly (eds), *Political Thinkers: From Socrates to the Present* (Oxford: Oxford University Press, 2003).

Ferguson, W. K., 'Humanistic views of the Renaissance', *American Historical Review*, XLV (1939–40).

Finocchiaro, M. A., *Galileo on the World Systems: A New Abridged Translation and Guide* (Berkeley: University of California Press, 1997).

Fontana, B., *Hegemony and Power: On the Relation between Gramsci and Machiavelli* (Minneapolis: University of Minnesota Press, 1993).

Freeman, D., *The Fateful Hoaxing of Margaret Mead: A Historical Analysis of her Samoan Research* (Boulder, Col.: Westview Press, 1999).

Garin, E., *Dal Rinascimento all'Illuminismo* (Pisa: Nistri-Lischi Editori, 1970).

——, *Italian Humanism: Philosophy and Civic Life in the Renaissance*, trans. P. Munz (Westport, Conn.: Greenwood, 1975).

Geerken, J. H., 'Machiavelli studies since 1969', *Journal of the History of Ideas*, 37 (1976).

Gilbert, A. H., *Machiavelli's 'Prince' and its Forerunners: 'The Prince' as a typical Book de regimine principium* (Durham, NC: Duke University Press, 1938).

Gilbert, F., *Machiavelli and Guicciardini* (Princeton: Princeton University Press, 1965).

——, 'The humanist concept of the prince and "The Prince" of Machiavelli', *The Journal of Modern History*, XI (1939).

Gramsci, A., *Quaderni del carcere*, ed. V. Gerratana (Turin: Einaudi, 1975), 4 vols.

Greer, S., *The Logic of Social Inquiry* (Chicago: Aldine Publishing Co., 1969).

Guicciardini, F., *Dialogo e discorsi del reggimento di Firenze*, ed. R. Palmarocchi (Bari: Laterza, 1932).

——, *Maxims and Reflections of a Renaissance Statesman*, trans. M. Domandi (New York: Harper & Row, 1965).

——, 'Considerations on the "Discourses" of Machiavelli', in *Selected Writings*, trans. and eds C. and M. Grayson (London: Oxford University Press, 1965).

Hale, J. R., *Machiavelli and Renaissance Italy* (London: English Universities Press, 1961).

Hancock, W. K., 'Machiavelli in modern dress: an enquiry into historical method', *History*, 20 (1935–6).

Hankins, J., 'Humanism and the origins of modern political thought', in

J. Kraye (ed.), *The Cambridge Companion to Renaissance Humanism* (Cambridge and New York: Cambridge University Press, 1996).

Hannaford, I., 'Machiavelli's concept of *virtù* in *The Prince* and the *Discourses* reconsidered', *Political Studies*, 20 (1972).

Hay, D., *The Italian Renaissance in its Historical Background* (Cambridge: Cambridge University Press, 1977).

Hexter, J. H., 'The Renaissance again – and again', *The Journal of Modern History*, 23 (1951).

Hobbes, T., *Leviathan*, ed. J. Plamenatz (London: The Fontana Library, 1962).

Hulliung, M., *Citizen Machiavelli* (Princeton: Princeton University Press, 1983).

Hume, D., *A Treatise of Human Nature*, bk. I, ed. D. G. C. Macnabb (London: The Fontana Library, 1962).

Jacobitti, E., *Revolutionary Humanism and Historicism in Modern Italy* (New Haven and London: Yale University Press, 1981).

Johnson, P., *The Renaissance: A Short History* (New York: Modern Library, 2000).

Kahn, V., *Machiavellian Rhetoric from the Counter-Reformation to Milton* (Princeton: Princeton University Press, 1994).

Keeley, L., *War before Civilization: The Myth of the Peaceful Savage* (New York: Oxford University Press, 1996).

Kraft, J., 'Truth and poetry in Machiavelli', *Journal of Modern History*, XXIII (1951).

Kristeller, P. O., *Renaissance Thought: The Classic, Scholastic, and Humanist Strains* (New York: Harper & Row, 1961).

——, 'The philosophy of Man in the Italian Renaissance', *Italica*, XXIV (1947).

Kuhn, T., *The Copernican Revolution* (Cambridge, Mass.: Harvard University Press, 1957).

Kymlicka, W., *Contemporary Political Philosophy: An Introduction* (Oxford: Clarendon Press, 1990).

Lukes, S., 'Marxism and dirty hands', in *Moral Conflict and Politics* (Oxford: Clarendon Press, 1991).

MacIntyre, A., *A Short History of Ethics* (London: Routledge & Kegan Paul, 1967).

Madison, J., 'Federalist no. 10', in A. Hamilton, J. Madison and J. Jay, *Selections from the Federalist*, ed. H. S. Commager (New York: Appleton-Century-Crofts, Inc., 1949).

Mansfield, H. C., *Machiavelli's Virtue* (Chicago: University of Chicago Press, 1998).

Marx, K., 'Economic and philosophic manuscripts' (1844), in *Writings of the Young Marx on Philosophy and Society*, eds and trans. L. D. Easton and K. H. Guddat (New York: Doubleday, 1967).

Mattingly, G., *Renaissance Diplomacy* (London: Cape, 1955).

Meinecke, F., *Machiavellism: The Doctrine of Raison d'État and its Place in Modern History*, trans. D. Scott (New Haven: Yale University Press, 1957).

Merleau-Ponty, M., *Humanism and Terror*, trans. J. O'Neill (Boston: Beacon Press, 1969).

Minogue, K., 'Method in intellectual history: Quentin Skinner's *Foundations*', in J. Tully (ed.), *Meaning and Context: Quentin Skinner and his Critics* (Cambridge: Polity Press, 1988).

Mosca, G., 'Il "Principe" di Machiavelli quattro secoli dopo la morte del suo autore', in *Ciò che la storia potrebbe insegnare* (Milan: Giuffrè, 1958). First published in 1927.

——, *The Ruling Class*, trans. H. D. Kahn (New York: McGraw Hill, 1939).

——, *Partiti e sindacati nella crisi del regime parlamentare* (Bari: Laterza, 1949).

Murray, P., and Murray, L., *The Art of the Renaissance* (London: Thames and Hudson, 1963).

O'Brien, C. C., 'The ferocious wisdom of Machiavelli', in *The Suspecting Glance* (London: Faber and Faber, 1972).

Olschki, L., *Machiavelli the Scientist* (Berkeley: The Gillick Press, 1945).

Parel, A. J., *The Machiavellian Cosmos* (New Haven and London: Yale University Press, 1992).

Pareto, V., *The Mind and Society*, trans. A. Bongiorno and A. Livingstone (London: Jonathan Cape, 1935), 4 vols.

Pinker, S., *The Blank Slate: The Modern Denial of Human Nature* (London: Penguin, 2002).

Plamenatz, J., 'Machiavelli', in *Man and Society*, vol. 1 (London: Longmans, 1968).

Plumb, J. H., *The Italian Renaissance* (New York: American Heritage Library, 1989).

Pocock, J. G. A., *The Machiavellian Moment: Florentine Political Thought and the Atlantic Republican Tradition* (Princeton: Princeton University Press, 1975).

——, 'Custom and grace, form and matter: an approach to Machiavelli's concept of innovation', in M. Fleisher (ed.), *Machiavelli and the Nature of Political Thought* (London: Croom Helm, 1973).

Pompanazzi, P., 'On the immortality of the soul', in E. Cassirer, P. O. Kristeller and J. H. Randall Jr. (eds and trans.), *The Renaissance Philosophy of Man: Selections in Translation* (Chicago, 1948).

Praz, M., 'Machiavelli and the Elizabethans', *Proceedings of the British Academy*, 13 (1928).

Prezzolini, G., *Machiavelli anticristo* (Rome: Casini, 1954).

Price, R., '*Ambizione* in Machiavelli's thought', *History of Political Thought*, 3 (1982).

Quinton, A., *Utilitarian Ethics* (London: Duckworth, 1973).

Rahe, P. A., *Republics Ancient and Modern: Classical Republicanism and the American Tradition* (Chapel Hill: University of North Carolina Press, 1992).

——, 'Situating Machiavelli', in J. Hankins (ed.), *Renaissance Civic Humanism* (Cambridge: Cambridge University Press, 2000).

Ridolfi, R., *The Life of Niccolò Machiavelli*, trans. C. Grayson (Chicago: University of Chicago Press, 1963).

Rousseau, J. J., *The Social Contract and Discourses*, trans. and ed. G. D. H. Cole (London: J. M. Dent & Sons, 1966).

Rubinstein, N., *The Government of Florence under the Medici 1434–1494* (Oxford: Oxford University Press, 1966).

Russo, L., *Machiavelli* (Bari: Laterza, 1949).

Sasso, G., *Il pensiero politico di Niccolò Machiavelli* (Turin: ERI Edizioni RAI, 1964).

Singleton, C. S., 'The perspective of art', *The Kenyon Review*, XV (1953).

Skinner, Q., *Machiavelli* (Oxford: Oxford University Press, 1981).

——, 'The paradoxes of political liberty', in S. M. McMurrin (ed.), *The Tanner Lectures on Human Values*, vol. VII (Cambridge and London: Cambridge University Press, 1986).

——, 'Machiavelli's *Discorsi* and the pre-humanist origins of republican ideas', in G. Bock, Q. Skinner and M. Viroli (eds), *Machiavelli and Republicanism* (Cambridge: Cambridge University Press, 1990).

Sowell, T., *A Conflict of Visions* (New York: William Morrow, 1987).

Strauss, L., *Thoughts on Machiavelli* (Chicago and London: University of Chicago Press, 1958).

Sullivan, V. B., 'Machiavelli's momentary "Machiavellian moment": a reconsideration of Pocock's treatment of the *Discourses*', *Political Theory*, 20 (1992).

Viroli, M., *Machiavelli* (Oxford: Oxford University Press, 1998).

——, 'Machiavelli and the republican idea of politics' in G. Bock, Q. Skinner and M. Viroli (eds), *Machiavelli and Republicanism* (Cambridge: Cambridge University Press, 1990).

Walzer, M., 'Political action: the problem of dirty hands', *Philosophy and Public Affairs*, 2 (1973).

Warren, M. E. (ed.), *Democracy and Trust* (Cambridge: Cambridge University Press, 1999).

Whitfield, J. H., *Machiavelli* (New York: Russell and Russell, 1965).

Wolin, S. S., *Politics and Vision: Continuity and Innovation in Western Political Thought* (London: Allen & Unwin Ltd., 1961).

Wood, G. S., *The Creation of the American Republic* (Chapel Hill: University of North Carolina Press, 1969).

Wood, N., 'The value of asocial sociability: contributions of Machiavelli, Sidney and Montesquieu', in M. Fleisher (ed.), *Machiavelli and the Nature of Political Thought* (London: Croom Helm, 1973).

Wrangham, R. W., and Peterson, D., *Demonic Males: Apes and the Origins of Human Violence* (Boston: Houghton Mifflin, 1996).

Zolo, D., *Democracy and Complexity* (Cambridge: Polity Press, 1992).

Index